Queen Mary's Book
for India

Fr.

Queen Mary's Book

FOR INDIA

WITH A FOREWORD BY
THE RIGHT HON. L. S. AMERY M.P.

GEORGE G. HARRAP & CO. LTD.
LONDON TORONTO BOMBAY SYDNEY

First published 1943
by GEORGE G. HARRAP & CO. LTD.
182 High Holborn, London, W.C.1

THIS BOOK IS PRODUCED IN
COMPLETE CONFORMITY WITH THE
AUTHORIZED ECONOMY STANDARDS

Set in Imprint type and printed by R. & R. CLARK, LIMITED, *Edinburgh*
Made in Great Britain

MARLBOROUGH HOUSE
S.W.I.

I send this message to the mothers of India's
fighting men:-

"You are constantly in my thoughts and
"I know that many of you are anxious, and some are
"sorrowful, but all are proud of your brave sons.
"My own dear sons have served in the Navy, Army and
"Air Force and I share your anxieties, your sorrows,
"and your pride.   I do not forget the patient
"fortitude of your daughters-in-law and I trust that
"your gentle care sustains them in this time of trial.
"I pray that God may bless all gallant Indian soldiers,
"sailors, and airmen and that in the hour of victory
"they may return with great honour to their homes
"and make your hearts glad again."

Mary R

1942

ACKNOWLEDGMENTS

THE thanks of the Editors are due in the first place to the contributors to the book, who have allowed entirely gratuitously the use of the articles and poems which appear below their names throughout the volume, and to Sir Bruce Richmond for valuable help in the final arrangement of the book. Specific acknowledgment should also be made to the following:

Messrs Constable and Co., Ltd., for " Vae Victori," from *Turn Fortune*, by Hugh Lyon; the Editor of the *Daily Telegraph*, for " A Sepoy Looks at the War," by " Rasp "; the Oxford University Press, for " The Shepherd," from *The Alert*, by Wilfrid Gibson, and for a passage from *Loyalties*, by Sir Arnold Wilson, K.C.I.E., C.S.I., C.M.G.; and the Editor of the *Sunday Times*, for " To an Indian Airman," by G. Rostrevor Hamilton.

FOREWORD

THIS little book, prefaced by the human touch of the Queen Mother's message to the mothers of India's fighting men and happily bearing Queen Mary's name, is mainly about India. More particularly is it concerned with India's share in the world conflict and with the men and women of India who are playing so splendid a part in our common cause. It is also for India, inasmuch as the profits derived from its sale have been dedicated to the Indian Comforts Fund by Miss Cornelia Sorabji, whose glowing patriotism, for India and for the Empire, and indefatigable energy, unquenched by years, have been responsible for the conception and for the carrying out of the work.

India has her own long tradition of martial valour. From the days of Alexander's chivalrous opponent, King Porus, onward her story has been rich in heroic exploits, in stubborn endurance, and in self-sacrificing loyalty. Hindu and Moslem, Rajput, Sikh and Maratha, Gurkha from the Himalayas and Madrassi from the far south— her varied races have all in their day gallantly played their part on the field of battle. Their traditions have lived on in the historic regiments of the British Indian Army, as well as in the forces of the Indian States. To-day that tradition is being enriched and broadened by the bravery and skilled efficiency of the young Indian officers, drawn from every part of India, who have won such a good name for themselves under the exacting test of modern war, and to whom India must increasingly look for her future security.

Never in her history, not even in the last war, has India made an effort comparable either in volume or in quality with that which she is making to-day. She has raised a million and a half soldiers, every man a volunteer. She has contributed to the sea war a Navy ever growing in numbers and efficiency, as well as the indispensable service of some forty thousand merchant seamen. Her own pilots, manning her own Air Force, are beginning to play an effective part in the latest field of war. She has contributed, on a scale undreamt of in the past, to the modern equipment of her own forces as well as to the whole Allied war effort in the field of supplies of all kinds.

No less striking has been the contribution of her goodwill in the individual gifts which, from the wealthiest Princes to the poorest peasant, have poured in through the Viceroy's Fund to mark India's appreciation of our own efforts and sacrifices here, whether for the squadrons of the Royal Air Force or for the victims of the enemy's attack upon our homes. It is a good-will matched by equal good-will towards India here. Only the other day an appeal by the High Commissioner for the sufferers from the Midnapore cyclone met with an immediate response in the shape of some £23,000 contributed in a few days. The Indian Comforts Fund itself represents the conjunction of that good-will in the donations received from both sides and in the devoted work which it has enlisted here. It is that same mutual good-will—the only true secret to the solution of India's problems—which has inspired the Editors and the contributors of this little book, for which I wish all the success it so well deserves.

February 1943

8

CONTENTS

Part I : *India in War-time*

Part II : *Anthology—Mainly about India*

9

ILLUSTRATIONS

Part I

INDIA IN WAR-TIME

*

10 DOWNING STREET

ALL depends now upon the whole life-strength of the British race in every part of the world and of all our associated peoples and of all well-wishers in every land doing their utmost night and day, giving all, daring all, enduring all—to the utmost, to the end.

Winston S. Churchill

From a broadcast speech (July 14, 1940)

Tribute to the Indian Army

by

Field-Marshal Sir Archibald Wavell, G.C.B., C.M.G., M.C.
Commander-in-Chief, India

AS Commander-in-Chief, Middle East, I owed a deep debt of gratitude to the Indian Army and to the Indian people for all the invaluable aid and support I received from them during the two years I was in command in the Middle East.

For more than a year after the outbreak of war the 4th Indian Division with the 7th Armoured Division formed the main, almost the only, bulwark of the defence of Egypt; and it was these two divisions that in the beginning of December 1940 won the battle of Sidi Barrani, destroying five Italian divisions. A little earlier, in August, Indian troops had formed part of a gallant little force which in British Somaliland had resisted for many days the onslaught of a force four or five times superior in numbers and equipment and had successfully withdrawn after inflicting heavy loss on their enemy.

In the late autumn of 1940 the 5th Indian Division had been sent to reinforce the Sudan, where a garrison of three British battalions and the few and scattered companies of the Sudan Defence Force, without a single gun or armoured vehicle, had for several months been facing the great Italian armies in Eritrea and Abyssinia. The 5th Indian Division and the Sudanese troops, in spite of their numerical inferiority, so harried the Italian troops opposing them, both at Gallabat and on the Eritrean border, as to gain complete moral ascendancy. Directly the battle of Sidi Barrani was won I sent the 4th Indian Division to join the 5th in the Sudan. These two divisions, with the support of some Sudanese troops, carried out that brilliant campaign in Eritrea and Abyssinia of which Agordat, Barentu, Keren, Asmara, Massawa, and Amba Alagi mark the stages and

14

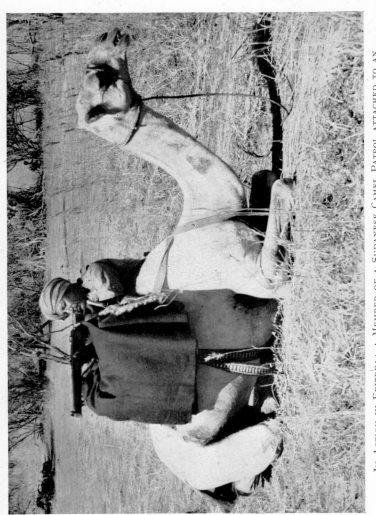

In Action in Eritrea: a Member of a Sudanese Camel Patrol attached to an Indian Infantry Brigade

14

A Bren-gun Carrier followed by Indian Infantry training in the Desert

victories. Farther south Indian troops from Aden took part in a skilful little operation leading to the recapture of Berbera and the reoccupation of British Somaliland.

Meanwhile an Indian Motor Brigade had been doing most gallant work in helping to stem the German counter-attack in Cyrenaica. Later the 4th Indian Division, its work in East Africa completed, was engaged in the Western Desert and in Syria, and in both theatres had again made a great contribution to success and enhanced the reputation of Indian troops. Again, when the situation in Iraq suddenly became critical in April 1941 it was troops from India who helped to restore our position there, and who subsequently assisted our occupation of Syria.

By this brief summary you will see how great a part troops from India, British and Indian, have played in the Middle East. And India has sent not only men but great quantities of material. On behalf of the Middle East, I once more thank India for her efforts.

Apart from the question of actual operations the presence of Indian troops in the Middle East has been of great benefit in their establishing a comradeship in arms with the troops of other parts of the Empire, practically all of whom were represented in the Middle East. I know also the good discipline and fine bearing of the Indian troops made a most favourable impression on the Egyptians.

On leaving the Middle East I was honoured by being appointed Commander-in-Chief in India and was thus able to see at first hand India's war effort in raising troops and making munitions both for forces overseas and for her own defence. It is an impressive effort both on the training-ground and in the workshops.

India herself has so far been spared the cruel experience of this destructive and ruthless war, thanks mainly to the troops she has sent overseas to keep the conflict at as great a distance from her frontiers as possible. Egypt, Syria, Aden, Iraq, Malaya, are bulwarks of India's own defence, and the campaign in East Africa was fought mainly to secure the line of communications between India and the Middle East. It is because the enemy has been kept at a distance that India has continued to enjoy immunity from air raids or invasion, from which so many other countries have suffered. Nevertheless India has made all preparations for her defence should the war come closer. Formidable defensive works have been constructed to bar the routes of invasion on the north-west land frontier, while the organization for air defence is being solidly built up.

When final victory comes, India will have played a proud part, befitting her great military traditions and her destiny.

A. P. Wavell
General
Cmil India

October 1941

INDIANS ON DUTY WITH A BREN GUN IN THE WESTERN DESERT

A Meeting of Old and Young Soldiers of the King-Emperor in the Desert

A Punjabi Seaman of the Indian Royal Navy
He is handling twin Lewis guns.

Tribute to the Royal Indian Navy

by

Commander Anthony Kimmins

THE last time I came into close contact with the Royal Indian Marine (as it was then called) was shortly after the Great War. As we steamed into Bombay various R.I.M. depot and training ships, with their white sides and yellow funnels, were lying at anchor. Later—during two and a half years' service in the Persian Gulf—we constantly came into contact with some of the smaller ships which were up there on their various duties.

I remember at the time being most impressed by the officers and ships' companies of these ships and by how favourably they compared with our own standards of naval efficiency, in spite of the fact that their principal duties— surveying and the inspection of lights and other aids to mariners—were of a more peaceful nature than ours.

It was not until 1934 that the Bill was finally passed to reorganize the Royal Indian Marine as a combatant Service and rename it the Royal Indian Navy, so that there was only a period of some five years before the outbreak of the present war in which to build up an experienced body of officers and men fully trained in all the developments of modern warfare.

In our own Navy it takes a considerable number of years to train a naval officer before he is considered fit to go to sea and take his place in one of our active-service warships. After that there is a long period of gaining experience afloat before he can be entrusted to any position of responsibility. Once having achieved that position, a large proportion are again required for the many highly specialized branches of modern naval warfare. This again means more years of study and experience. The same applies in a lesser degree to the naval rating.

While some of these specialized branches, such as the

submarines and the Fleet Air Arm, are not as yet required in the R.I.N there are many highly specialized branches, such as gunnery, torpedo, signalling, and mine-sweeping (to quote only a few), which are absolutely essential for the protection of India's long coast-line.

To me it is a source of constant wonder that the present high state of efficiency of to-day's Royal Indian Navy could have been achieved in the few years since its formation as a fighting Service. How that state of efficiency has been reached is a mystery which only some one who has served in the R.I.N. can answer, but the fact that it does exist is plainly evident from the many successes achieved by the R.I.N. during the present war.

In 1940 five sloops of the R.I.N. were placed under the command of the Commander-in-Chief, East Indies, for service in the Red Sea, Gulf of Aden, and Persian Gulf. After valuable service in these waters they proceeded to play an important part in the operations which led to the downfall of the Italian Empire in East Africa and later in the brief Iran campaign.

March 16, 1941, will always be remembered as a historic day in the annals of the R.I.N., for on it the first combined operation between units of the Indian Army and the R.I.N. took place. This was the reoccupation of Berbera.

In the early hours warships and troop-carriers, together with a number of tankers and lighters, appeared within a mile of the British Somaliland coast. Amongst the warships were H.M.I.S. *Netravati* and *Parvati*, which had taken part in the evacuation of the garrison from British Somaliland in August of the preceding year. Now, on their return visit in happier circumstances, they and other ships of the R.I.N. carried out a heavy bombardment and silenced the Italian shore batteries and provided covering fire for landing-parties.

During the advance of our forces from the Sudan into Eritrea the R.I.N. played a vitally important part in maintaining by sea the supply base of the Indian Army force which was able to push in from the coast on to the left flank of the Italian position at Keren and so take the Italians entirely by surprise.

Later, on April 8, when the final attack on Massawa began, British and Indian warships appeared out of the dawn and felt their way through the mine-infested waters. Their appearance again took the Italians entirely by surprise and resulted in the flight and subsequent scuttling of the Italian warships in harbour.

These and other similar operations removed for a time the main threat to India's shipping in home waters, and their success, in spite of the treacherous coast-line and enemy minefields, proved conclusively the high standard of efficiency in to-day's R.I.N.

To-day there is another and far greater threat to Indian waters, but—whatever the result—there is little doubt that the R.I.N. will add many a glorious page to its history.

Anthony Kimmins

Tribute to Indian Airmen

by

Acting Air Marshal Sir Patrick Playfair,
K.B.E., C.B., C.V.O., M.C.

NO part of the British Empire has given more convincing proof of its determination to play its full part in the Battle for Freedom than India.

Not only in Libya, Abyssinia, and the Far East have her sons fought with matchless brilliance and courage, but in another element—in the skies above Britain and over India and Burma—they have shown themselves true partners in the great brotherhood of the R.A.F.

To-day India has her own Air Force. The first squadron was formed in 1933, within a few weeks of Adolf Hitler's assumption of the Chancellorship of the Third Reich. The Commanding Officer and the N.C.O.'s were ' lent ' by the R.A.F., but the Indian officers were trained at the Royal Air Force College at Cranwell, and other ranks, recruited from all over India, at the Aircraft Depot, Karachi. Indian pilots took to flying with the same zest as to polo and other ground sports, in which they have always excelled.

In a remarkably short space of time these young pilots and ground-crews took their place alongside R.A.F. squadrons. Their high standard of flying and maintenance earned the praise of successive Air Officers Commanding in India.

The squadron's primary duty was army co-operation, and detached flights flew all over India to carry out training with Indian Army units.

At the outbreak of war the Indian Air Force was barely six years old. Much valuable experience had already been gained by its personnel when the hour came for more rapid expansion. A Service Flying Training School, an Initial Training Centre, and a School of Technical Training were established in India. In addition a number of Indian pilots were seconded for duty with the R.A.F. in England and were among the famous " few " in the Battle of Britain.

Indian students in England rallied to R.A.F. recruiting-offices by the score. To-day they are taking part in the mass raids on industrial Germany, and some of them are flying in the fastest machines in the world. One young Indian pilot, son of a High Court judge of Bombay, sank a large Nazi ship. He was flying a Beaufort torpedo-bomber on his third operational flight. Another young Indian has bombed Berlin twice. The list of awards granted to young pilots and R.A.F. personnel born in India continues to grow. Many are doing vitally important jobs on the ground—the technicians and others who keep aircraft in fighting trim.

When Japan started to spread over Asia, and when the gateway to India, most glittering prize of all, was threatened, it was decided to send No. 1 Squadron of the Indian Air Force to Burma. It was followed by a second squadron, and both were not only commanded by Indians but almost completely manned by Indians. The two squadrons, flying alongside the R.A.F. and the American Volunteer Group, fought with unflinching courage and determination, earning the highest praise from General Wavell.

The growth and expansion of the Indian Air Force goes steadily forward, and already there are nearly ten complete squadrons, with a continuous flow of pilots and mechanics in reserve. The day is near when the Indian Air Force will take over a considerable portion of the R.A.F. ground organization in India, and a further step forward in its career was marked recently by the presentation of a General Badge and Ensign by the Duke of Gloucester in the name of the King-Emperor.

No brief survey of India's part in the air war against the Axis would be complete without reference to the famed squadrons of Fighter and Bomber Commands, bearing Indian crests and names, which have contributed a full share in the R.A.F.'s glorious record of achievement. Prince and peasant have given with a generosity which reveals the united aim of India to fight the forces of evil wherever they may be found. They have given over £4,000,000 for the purchase of fighter and bomber planes for the R.A.F. in individual gifts ranging from a few annas to cheques for £150,000.

The two Hyderabad squadrons have together shot down more than a hundred aircraft in the defence of Great Britain. The giant Halifaxes presented by the people of Madras have taken part in many of the heavy raids on the Ruhr and the Rhineland, while fighters presented by the same generous donors, together with others bearing the crests of the United Provinces, of Calcutta, Bengal, Bombay, and the warrior races of the Punjab, are also playing their part.

These are some of the signs and portents of the new India which is rising up to meet her destiny. Never before have so many castes, creeds, and races been united in one single endeavour as they are in the Indian Air Force. " In Unity there is Strength " is the motto of India's No. 1 Squadron. That unity and comradeship is impressively shown in the friendly relations between the Indian Air Force and the Royal Air Force in India, no less than in the presence of Hindus, Muslims, Sikhs, Parsees, and Bengalis among the personnel of the I.A.F.

Patrick H. L. Playfair

The Labour-training Scheme for India

by

The Right Hon. Ernest Bevin, P.C., M.P.
Minister of Labour and National Service

THE great thing to strive for in the modern world is speedily to raise the standard of life of the masses. Independently of political considerations, the essential thing for India is to improve the conception of the people of what life ought to yield and to provide opportunities for its realization.

India has at her disposal all the resources necessary to give her the greatest opportunity in the world for orderly and yet speedy advancement. At the same time her people need industries, more purchasing power, and the development of their skill in modern production.

If the standard of living of India is raised it will not be a question of competition with us but actually increasing the people's standards of consumption and making them better customers for the rest of the world.

The war has brought out in very strong relief the necessity for industry to be developed. India has the greatest reserve of man-power in the Commonwealth. The Government, therefore, took the view that it was essential to bring Indians to this country in order that they might have an opportunity for training in the art of production and be introduced to the responsibilities of supervision, and thus return to their own country with a better understanding of what is necessary if they are to develop their own industrial techniques.

We have also introduced them to the best methods known to us for the organization and development of trade unions, the methods of book-keeping and conduct of their branches, of negotiation and the system of wage-fixing.

With the knowledge they have obtained we have every reason to hope that these young men will accept positions of responsibility and play their full part in assisting the masses of India to develop stable organizations.

Then we have sent a number of instructors and technicians from here to India, and so the methods that have been adopted have been reciprocal.

To sum up, our object in inaugurating this scheme was twofold—first, to make an immediate contribution to help the war, and secondly, to impart the most knowledge we can with a view to assisting India to develop on an orderly and progressive basis. War-time conditions have, of necessity, forced the scheme to be kept within modest proportions, but none the less it offers great possibilities for mutual help now and for far-reaching development later.

Ernest Bevin

Tales of Indian Valour on all Fronts

BY December 1940 Indian troops—sappers and mechanized cavalry—are reported as taking a prominent part in the operations in Eritrea, doing as brilliantly in co-operation with British infantry and the Sudan Defence Forces as they did in the early stages of operations in the desert.

Punjab, Garhwal, Baluch, and Frontier Forces regiments fought throughout this Sudan-Abyssinian campaign—sappers clearing the road blocked with boulders and landmines by the retreating Italians, and making a way through narrow gorges in steeply mountainous country.

The story of one famous Indian regiment, now mechanized, must be told in detail as an example of the capabilities of Indian troops fighting in terrain to which they are accustomed.

For months before the offensive began the regiment was installed behind the British front line in a deep *wadi* in the Western Desert, working hard at strengthening defences, and being trained in desert warfare: devoted and tireless, accustoming themselves to sandstorms and every form of desert hardship—on one occasion, even rejoicing on being dive-bombed as they moved up to camp. " Good practice ! " A military officer reports:

Indian regiments in the desert appeared to be the best dug in, the best concealed; little sign of their presence could be seen as one approached them even at a distance of a few hundred yards. All their most important dugouts were approached through innocent-looking holes in the rock. Indians were probably the most comfortable troops in the desert, partly because their long experience of warfare of all sorts and conditions made them highly adaptable, and partly because, as is their custom, they bring their own camp-followers, tailors, bakers, etc., who are attached to the regiment. Many of the fine Indian troops one saw in the Western Desert were sons or grandsons of past members of the regiment, which has traditions going back to India's history of the last century.

And when the offensive began in December 1940 General Wavell decided that the Indians should be among the picked troops sent against Mussolini's desert expert at Malatti headquarters—the spot chosen by the enemy from which to invade Egypt.

After fighting throughout the initial desert blitz they concentrated on the dangerous work of removing the Italian mines along the coast, and clearing the road which runs between Mersa Matruh and Sidi Barrani in order that vital British services should get through. The Indian Signal Corps also worked with the advance line, establishing communications.

The awards of this period emphasize the gallantry of the men. Second-Lieutenant Premchandra Singh Bhagat, Corps of Indian Engineers (serving with the Royal Bombay Sappers and Miners), has the distinction of being the first Indian to receive the V.C. in this war (Deed of January 31/ February 1, 1941):

> For most conspicuous gallantry on active service in the Middle East. During the pursuit of the enemy following the capture of Metemma on the night 31st January/1st February, 1941, Second-Lieutenant Bhagat was in command of a section of a Field Company, Sappers and Miners, detailed to accompany the leading mobile troops (Bren carriers) to clear the road and adjacent areas of mines. For a period of four days and over a distance of fifty-five miles this officer in the leading carrier led the column. He detected and supervised the clearing of fifteen minefields. Speed being essential, he worked at high pressure from dawn to dusk each day. On two occasions when his carrier was blown up with casualties to others, and on a third occasion when ambushed and under close enemy fire, he himself carried straight on with his task. He refused relief when worn out with strain and fatigue and with one ear-drum punctured by an explosion, on the grounds that he was now better qualified to continue his task to the end.
>
> His coolness, persistence over a period of ninety-six hours, and gallantry, not only in battle, but throughout the long period when the safety of the column and the speed at which it would advance were dependent on his personal efforts, were of the highest order.

Another V.C. recipient was Subhadar Richpal Ram, 6th Rajputana Rifles (Deed of February 7/8, 1941):

During the assault on enemy positions in front of Keren, Eritrea, on the night of 7/8th February, 1941, Subhadar Richpal Ram, who was second-in-command of a leading company, insisted on accompanying the forward platoon and led its attack on the first objective with great dash and gallantry. His company commander being then wounded, he assumed command of the company, and led the attack of the remaining two platoons to the final objective. In face of heavy fire, some thirty men with this officer at their head rushed the objective with the bayonet and captured it. The party was completely isolated, but under the inspiring leadership of Subhadar Richpal Ram, it beat back six enemy counter-attacks between midnight and 04.30 hours. By now ammunition had run out, and this officer extricated his command and fought his way back to his battalion with a handful of survivors through the surrounding enemy.

Again, in the attack on the same position on 12th February, this officer led the attack of his company. He pressed on fearlessly and determinedly in the face of heavy and accurate fire, and by his personal example inspired his company with his resolute spirit until his right foot was blown off. He then suffered further wounds from which he died. While lying wounded he continued to wave his men on, and his final words were, " We'll capture the objective."

The heroism, determination, and devotion to duty shown by this officer were beyond praise, and provided an inspiration to all who saw him.

Major Raj Kumar Rajendra Singh, 2nd Royal Lancers, Indian Army, was the first Indian commissioned officer ever to receive the D.S.O. He brought a detachment of sixty, all ranks, out of the engagement at Mekili on April 8/9, 1941, displaying initiative and leadership of the highest order in action and in the personal reconnaissances made the night before. His coolness and general demeanour throughout had a noticeable effect on the troops—both British and Indian.

The story behind this award has often been told—the story of the daring rush through the enemy's position, the capture of prisoners, and the final arrival at Headquarters after driving continuously for more than thirty hours right round the enemy on the desert flank. " It was a wonderful combination " (says the official record) " of determination, great leadership, and brilliant navigation." Major Rajendra Singh is a nephew of the late Jamsaheb of Nawanagar (" Ranji," the cricketer).

Lieutenant (Temporary Captain) Anant Singh Pattiani, 13th Frontier Force Rifles, Indian Army, received the M.C. On March 17, 1941, when commanding a flank company he was heavily attacked by at least a battalion of the enemy using mortars, light mortars, and grenades.

When the enemy succeeded in penetrating the centre of his section he led his company headquarters and the few men he had collected to the counter-attack. Blinded in one eye, wounded in the legs, he continued to lead, firing at the enemy with his pistol at a few yards range.

The enemy withdrew—the company's position was re-established. He continued to command his company for another five hours, until ordered to the rear by a senior officer.

The official report says his action undoubtedly prevented the development of a serious situation.

Out of the mass of interesting detail and a saga of deeds of valour the tale next set down is selected because it is unique. It is the story of the capture of an Italian island in the Red Sea by the combined operation of a sloop of the R.I.N. and a few men of the Maratha Light Infantry.

One morning at the end of April 1941 a party of Marathas went aboard a sloop in Masaba harbour, setting out for the island of Mokra.

White flags greeted the sloop from every available flag-staff as soon as our guns were turned on the island. The party went ashore for a parley. They found about nine hundred Germans and Italians collected to be shipped as prisoners to Massawa. The British demand for surrender of all money on the island was met by a wail that there had long been no money. No wages had been paid for many months. A search showed empty safes, and the Governor's word was accepted. But an Italian prisoner with a grudge against the Governor revealed the fact that he and some Blackshirts were escaping with treasure from the other side of the island.

A dhow went in pursuit and finally captured the fugitives —the Governor, a general, two colonels, various A.D.C.'s, *and* many canvas bags of Maria Theresa dollars. The prisoners and the prize were soon safely aboard the R.I.N. sloop.

And here to end this campaign are a few details about the epic of Keren. The official record says, " After weary fighting for nearly a fortnight, under the most difficult conditions of climate and country, British and Indian troops admirably supported by the R.A.F. have again defeated a numerically superior enemy force and occupied Keren." Difficult they certainly were. Only men of courage, determination, and superb physical fitness could have fought month after month in a shade temperature of 105 degrees, thousands of feet up in the mountains or sweltering in the valleys, opposed by the cream of the Italian forces in Eritrea entrenched in positions selected with care and fortified at leisure. The capture of fortresses on the edge of the Eritrean foothills cleared the way for the advance on Keren, " a natural fortress set amid a fantastic jumble of soaring hills." Along a road dominated from the heights up and over the peaks themselves the Indian troops fought their way to victory. For more than a month the battle had swayed to and fro on mountain peaks and precipitous slopes.

" In such fighting," was the Military comment, " training, discipline, and perfect understanding between officers and men came into their own." And none of the Indians wounded or killed were ever left in No-man's-land. The value of this fact will be appreciated.

If for the civilian observer the deductions to be drawn from the early Desert and Libyan campaigns is that training, discipline, and self-restraint make the best foundation for dash, initiative, and leadership when dire necessity calls, the general comment made on the Malayan period is that this fact has been proved true, not only of the actual fighters, but of the non-combatant adjuncts of the Army also—of the medical unit, stretcher-bearers included ; of mechanics, signalmen, telephonists, and all those who maintain communications; and of the drivers, the washermen, and baggage-carriers who bring up the rear, and even the mules themselves. Here are a few of the tales which illustrate this fact—taken from a bulky record of deeds of valour. For example, there was the stretcher-bearer who, surrounded by the enemy when bringing in a wounded sepoy, seized the sepoy's rifle and beat off the assailants single-handed—taking his burden safely to camp.

Or the tale of the body of Indians attacked by heavy machine-gun fire as they approached the enemy's outer defences. A sepoy was hit in the chest and fell, but managed to get his gun into firing position and to go on firing into the enemy gun position till he died.

Or this of the Rajput soldier commanding a platoon who, wounded in the arm, continued to lead his men until hit in the leg, when, leaning against a tree, he hurled hand-grenades against the enemy, until again wounded.

Another non-commissioned officer, leading his men through heavy artillery fire, was badly wounded in both legs. Compelled then to lie on a stretcher, he continued to cheer and enhearten them till he died. The whole campaign was punctuated with acts of gallantry and of loyalty to the brigade and to individuals of all ranks—for example, refusing to withdraw till outlying fighters were able to get to safety; single-handed assaults on the enemy; the initiative taken when stranded. . . .

The Mandi, Jammu, and Kangra troops fighting in the opening of the campaign were among those distinguished for courage in taking the initiative in tight corners, and for the ingenuity, coolness, and presence of mind which engineered daring escapes for such men as were taken prisoner.

Among the awards of this campaign were several I.D.S.M.'s (Indian Distinguished Service Medals).

Driver Devi Dyal, of the Jammu and Kishmir Artillery I.S.F., won his medal during operations in the Damascus Sector (July 11, 1941). The battery and wagon lines were being heavily shelled, and, as it was feared that mules which had broken loose would give away the position, drivers were ordered to catch the mules and lead them to better cover. While doing this Driver Devi Dyal was hit by a shell which severed his right arm. He continued to control his mule, which attempted to bolt, and led it to a trench, where he held it till he was evacuated, still protesting against not being allowed to carry on with his duty. Signalman Amar Singh, of the 4th Field Regiment, was in charge of an important telephone line. Disregarding the enemy's fire, he repaired it five times, maintaining vital communications. He was rewarded with the I.D.S.M. Many of these stories of gallantry and valour cover the first fortnight of the fighting. When attacked on the beaches the Dogras had a very narrow front and were concentrated in five posts which fought till their ammunition was exhausted. After this there were instances when the Dogras went for the invaders with hatchets; and one man is believed to have killed seven of the enemy. A Jemadar from Kangra rallied the troops on Badang beach, and attacked and counter-attacked from the early hours till nightfall, assisted by a Havildar, also from Kangra, commanding a carrier platoon. When ordered to withdraw, several of the posts refused to obey till their second-in-command and the above-mentioned Jemadar had themselves identified and verified the order.

The story of the brilliant dash through the Italian tank formation and the German Panzer columns supported by mechanized infantry is one of the high lights of the Indian Middle East campaign.

"You've got through because you were bold," said General Auchinleck; "be always bold." And of the brigade, "It would have been an almost impossible task in view of the enemy forces surrounding us, but for the coolness and intrepidity shown by the brigade as a whole and the firm determination to break through." The 4th Indian Division formed the spearhead of the Imperial Army's thrust into Cyrenaica from Tobruk onward. "Their discipline was excellent, and their behaviour both on the battlefield and on occupied enemy territory was exemplary," said General Ritchie.

To this division was entrusted in December 1941 the

task of ' mopping up ' the rough area between Barce and Benghazi.

Preliminary reports show that twenty-four aircraft have been destroyed by various units of the division. There were sixteen Junkers of various types, five Messerschmitts, a couple of Dorniers, and another. The number of prisoners captured by the 4th Division from November 23 is 122 officers and 4182 other ranks. And in addition approximately a thousand prisoners were taken at Giovanni Brota, while probably yet another thousand bypassed the division's counting-points.

The full story of the dashing attack by a battalion of the 11th Sikh Regiment on Derna aerodrome has lately been released and tops the pyramid of gallantry to the credit of Indian soldiers from all parts of that vast subcontinent and of all races and many occupations—volunteers all in the service of the King-Emperor, of country, and of the defence of the oppressed.

In North Africa the 4th Indian Division has taken part in the great advance of the Eighth Army from Egypt to Tunisia, and it is fitting that we should close this brief record of the work of the Indian Army with the message from the Prime Minister to the Viceroy of India which is published as the present book is passing through the press :

We have watched with admiration the splendid achievements of the 4th Indian Division in the Battle of Mareth and in the recent victory at Wadi Akarit. The high renown of India's soldiers and of the redoubtable Gurkha troops has been enhanced by the out-standing performance of the Indian Army in all the campaigns of the Middle East. I take this occasion to express to the Princes and peoples of India, and to our firm friend H.H. the Maharaja of Nepal, our admiration and gratitude for all that the Indian Army has done in Africa, in the Far East, and in India itself. We take pride that India's fighting men should now share in the successes which have crowned the long uphill contest in which they have played so valiant a part.

An Indian Bandsman

A Punjabi Pilot of the R.A.F.,
Middle East
He was one of the first Indian pilots to be
trained in Britain.

A Sepoy of the Rajputana Rifles,
from Jaipur State

Indian Sapper

India's War Effort

(i) THE ECONOMIC GROUP COUNCIL: EASTERN AREA

AN Eastern Group Conference representing sixteen countries was convened in October 1940 on the recommendation of H.E. the Viceroy. The sixteen countries represented at the Conference were—Australia, New Zealand, South Africa, India, Southern Rhodesia, Kenya, Uganda, Tanganyika, Northern Rhodesia, Nyasaland, Zanzibar, Burma, Ceylon, Hongkong, Malaya, and Palestine. The Eastern Group Council, outcome of the Conference, is a body welding together the industrial capacity of these sixteen countries.

The Council is in constant session, and through it the Governments join hands to improve the organization of war supplies to the Middle East, the Far East, and any place in which the Empire troops are stationed. It meets in Delhi, India. The policy is that as far as possible war supplies should be drawn from the home industrial area of any country in the group. It is therefore imperative, for example, for the Indian representative on the Council to keep in the closest touch with his own Indian Supply Department and with Indian industry. He may find that at any given moment India may not be able to meet her need; but as the Council sits in continuous session, and as the search goes on, India's industrial capacity is stimulated, enlarged, and fulfilled from month to month.

The like is the case with other countries. And upon the manner in which each country discharges this primal duty rests its value to the Council and to itself.

Next, upon information supplied to it about group capacity, the Council decides on the country to which a particular demand should be allocated. The Supply Department concerned carries out such a decision in the manner which it deems best.

The demand for war supplies is so great that at first it had to be met mainly by group countries acting together.

This situation is reported to be improving, with self-sufficiency for an aim. But where several countries have a surplusage of any particular article there is no rivalry with a view to individual profit; the Council decides the proportion in which supplies should be contributed. And, other things being equal, the country nearest to the area of need carries the load.

The scheme, in fact, is a pooling of resources as far as possible among the sixteen countries for the speedy winning of the war, with a keen watch on the saving of shipping and transport—where allocation is under consideration.

To quote Mr M. S. A. Hydari, Indian Member of the Council, " Its purpose is the efficient procurement of war supplies, using the Eastern group as a vast unit of supply. The end of the war should see an end of the Council as it is at present." But he suggests that the contacts which are being made and the spirit of understanding which is developed by our interrelated needs may well lead to peace-time collaboration beneficial to all.

This, then, is the setting in which Indian industrial war-time effort is being developed. What has it achieved so far? Where not only " soul " but visible effort must needs go " marching on," figures in a single survey such as this would never catch up with reality. Let us, therefore, look with more detail at what led up to the Council, so as to have wherewith to feed imagination from milestone to further milestone. The recommendation to modernize the Indian Army dates from the Chatfield Committee of 1938. This Committee recommended the expenditure on equipment of £34,000,000. Britain immediately supplied £30,000,000 of the amount to meet all necessary expenditure except that needed for the actual defence of India.

In July 1940 came Sir Alexander Roger's Ministry of Supply Mission, leading eventually to the Economic Council, and incidentally to the Purchasing Mission to America of 1941 under Sir Shanmukham Chetty. India had to buy what she could not yet supply for herself. Britain furnished the money.

Lease-Lend was extended to India, and brought Dr Grady's Technical American Mission to India to help explore possibilities. The decision was mass production. India was to be rationalized and regimented.

And this has already happened.

India is practically, in 1942, supplying her own military equipment in great measure. Some sixty thousand different articles are required by a modern army. India supplies more than forty-five thousand of these. And Sir Homi Mehta, the industrialist, Supply Member of the Government of India, tells us that India will reach the peak in munitions and ordnance factories by the middle of 1943. The number of ordnance factories and of skilled employees grows monthly. Similarly clothing equipment has risen from the seventy-five thousand garments produced in 1939 to seven million in 1942.

India has further forged ahead in other directions: textiles generally, both woollen and cotton; leather (three million boots and shoes a year, and sadlery and harness); metals and minerals (steel and iron in specially requisitioned form, platinum, and industrial diamonds); timber (production in 1942, 500,000 tons); medicinal drugs and stores; armoured vehicles; equipment for A.R.P. The production of foodstuffs is also receiving expert attention.

And India is supplying more than her own needs. Steel and iron are among her special contribution to Allied countries; and her textiles—cotton and woollen fabrics, blankets, material for parachutes—are in great demand.

Village hand-loom industries are being developed through Provincial control and can supply webbing, tapes, cordage, etc.

Examination of specific statistics show that India has sent textiles, canvas, foodstuffs, railway rolling-stock, timber, coal, etc. to the United Kingdom, Australia, New Zealand, East Africa, the Middle East, Singapore, and other places, besides munitions and war supplies to the Middle East, Iraq, and Iran. India is indeed doing her part.

And the end is not yet.

The " Bevin boys " are making a lasting difference to the entire industrial outlook—bringing to industry, with efficiency, the ideas of Western Trade Unionism and leadership, as well as higher standards of living, and the comradeship which ignores all differences of race or caste.

(ii) THE MILITARY FRONT

THE ARMY

BY reason of her geographical position India is now the pivot of the British area of defence. Her troops form part of the overseas expeditionary forces and garrisons in countries ranging from China to Libya and the Western Desert. They have served with their Dominion and American comrades in Malaya, Burma, Iran, Iraq, Syria, Palestine, East Africa, Abyssinia, Aden, and the Seychelles. Generals and commanders-in-chief have testified to their indomitable courage, efficiency, and resourcefulness, and that they also have the admiration and friendship of their Western comrades in arms was lately recorded in a broadcast by a British officer who served with Indian troops of all kinds in battle in Syria, Egypt, and Libya. He concluded, after describing their gallantry in specific engagements, and their reliability as friends in all circumstances:

I for one could wish for nothing better than to fight with my unit alongside these cheerful and courageous warriors. Their utter dependability to support their sister British battalion in a tight spot, in the past, is well known throughout the Middle East. This high standard will, I am convinced, be maintained wherever British and Indian troops find themselves together.

An Indian contingent has served with the British Expeditionary Forces in the Western European theatre of operations also, and has formed part of the Forces in Britain since its arrival there after the collapse of France. Of this body, formed in 1939, the Commandant, Lieutenant-Colonel R. S. Hills, M.C., writes, " It is almost if not quite unique, in that it consists of units one of which did not exist before the war."

He describes their life and training in France before the invasion of the Low Countries, and their gallantry during the historic evacuation from Dunkirk and elsewhere on the coast; their amazing dignity and resilience even in captivity; and at all times the happiness of the contacts made with other nationals.

Of the pre-invasion time in France he writes:

> The men became thoroughly popular with the French farmers: as smallholders in India they had much in common, and were interested in the French methods of farming, especially also in the stock. The French were most kind and hospitable, and in return the Indian soldiers helped the farmers as much as they could in their spare time. . . .
>
> Since the contingent arrived in Britain, they have been stationed in England, Scotland, and Wales. . . .
>
> At first the majority were in Derbyshire, where they were employed in preparing and manning defences against a possible invasion; but as many as could be spared helped the local farmers.

This friendly gesture was much appreciated both by the farmers — "The Indians worked three times as hard as our usual helpers," they said—and the parish generally. "By their bearing and determined methods," wrote the rector in the parish magazine, "the Indian troops have given great comfort at a time of grave national crisis."

"In Scotland they won good will by their respect for the religious observance of Sunday." Colonel Hills concludes:

> There is not a man who is not longing to give of his best for H.M. the King-Emperor and for his country. Evolution has been rapid, and whatever else the war may do, it has been of supreme benefit to India and to the other members of the British Commonwealth. All have learned the lesson of how splendid are the other components of the brotherhood of Democracy. So far as India is concerned it has proved that her sons can expand and still remain charming, delightful, and unspoiled.

It cannot be repeated too often that recruiting for the Army is and has always been on a voluntary basis. An

Indian soldier, broadcasting about the Indian Army on the same occasion as that cited above, said, " Indians have always been ready to volunteer for the Army. Since the war started recruiting figures have gone up by many hundreds per cent." His talk illustrates the close association of the Indian Army with the village life of India, from which most of the Army is recruited, mostly by veteran ex-soldiers—the *bap-dada* (fathers and grandfathers) of the villagers.

Indian States Forces. To the British-Indian Forces are added the stout-hearted and sturdy Highlanders of the Gurkha regiments, supplied by the independent Kingdom of Nepal, Britain's ally for nearly a hundred and forty years; and the Indian States Forces of all arms, serving beside their British-Indian comrades both at home and overseas—including among others the famous Bikanir Camel Corps; and infantry battalions from Mysore, Hyderabad, Kapurthala, Bhawalpur, and Jind.

And the garrison in Eritrea is in 1942 comprised mainly of units of the Indian States Forces.

THE ROYAL INDIAN NAVY

The Royal Indian Navy has a long history dating back to the East India Company's Marines. Manned by Indian as well as European officers and by Indian ratings, it is co-operating in the Battle of the Atlantic, and carrying out marine duties on the Indian Ocean, Red Sea, and Persian Gulf.

The expansion of the R.I.N. has necessitated an enlarged programme of building construction, as well as an increase in training facilities.

The *Baroda* and *Travancore* for Indian mine-sweeping and submarine-chasing are the latest additions to India's coastal defence, and were built entirely by Indian labour. The repair, refitting, or conversion of merchant ships to war-time uses, and the construction of floating docks for the Admiralty, are amongst India's latest undertakings. Recruitment to the R.I.N. is open to all parts of India:

the personnel increased in 1941 by over 50 per cent. in officers and 100 per cent. in ratings.

A junior boys' training school, H.M.I.S. *Dilawar*, is to be opened at Karachi next year.

Indian Merchant Service. Before the war some thirty-three thousand Indian seamen were serving on British ships. To-day the figure is not less than forty thousand. Whereas Indian seamen used to be employed chiefly on passenger liners and cargo boats trading to and from the East they are now serving in every type of craft (including armed cruisers) in all parts of the world. When a voyage will take them north of latitude 30° N. or south of latitude 30° S. special food and clothing are provided for them. Their conduct and efficiency under the hard and exacting conditions of war-time voyages have been as outstanding in this war as in the last. Many have lost their lives by enemy action, and others have fallen into enemy hands and are now in prison camps. But there is no lack of men to take their place, and, as more shipping comes into the long supply line to the East, so does the number of Indian seamen in the British Merchant Navy increase. Special arrangements have been made for their comfort and well-being during their spells ashore. Ten hostels have been established in the northern ports of the United Kingdom, supervised by Indian welfare officers.

Their courage and devotion to duty have been recognized by the award of decorations to a number of Indian seamen, two of whom have received the British Empire Medal.

THE INDIAN AIR FORCE

The Indian Air Force, which is quite separate from the Royal Air Force, came into being in 1932, after the first Indian cadets had been trained at the R.A.F. College at Cranwell. Its duties, as laid down, are to combine with the R.A.F. in operations on the North-West Frontier, and to assist the Army and Navy in the event of invasion.

Before the outbreak of the present war a proportion of its members had already had experience of active service

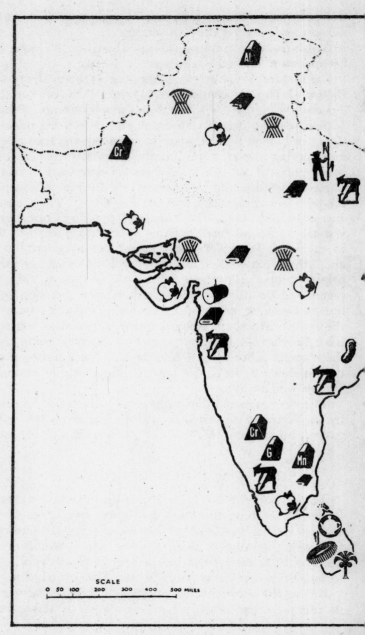

conditions on the North-West Frontier, where some of the most difficult terrain in the world is to be found.

Formed originally from a band of enthusiasts, most of whom had received their training at the hands of Indian members of civil flying-clubs in India, the Indian Air Force is expanding rapidly, and recruits are presenting themselves in steadily increasing numbers. Potential pilots and observers are available in large numbers, and on completion of their training recruits are being commissioned forthwith.

Though still in the training stage, the Indian Air Force is nevertheless being quickly developed with a view to taking over its full share of operational duties. At present responsibility for India's air defence rests primarily with the R.A.F.

Indians show great aptitude for flying, as was evidenced in the last war, when Indians served with distinction in the Royal Flying Corps, and later with the R.A.F. Many young Indians are serving to-day with the Royal Air Force, and a number of officers of the Indian Air Force, seconded to the R.A.F. for training, have already been taking part in operational flights over enemy territory; some of them have given their lives in the Empire's cause.

The first aeroplane assembled in India, a Harlow trainer, was test-flown last August at the Hindustan aircraft factory. This factory is also to build a Curtis fighter of the Hawk variety. Plans for the building of aeroplanes, with American help, are well advanced.

CIVIL DEFENCE SERVICES

The Civil Defence Services in India have been rapidly organized and developed. The possibility of air raids on her big cities in the event of a German break-through in the Caucasus and descent into Persia has been fully realized, and India will not be caught unprepared.

A Civil Defence Department, under an Indian Member of the Viceroy's Council, has been recently formed which, in co-ordination with the Provincial authorities, will be responsible for the preparation and organization of the whole population for possible air raids. Organizations for A.R.P. services are being drawn up in the Provinces, a roof-spotter system for vital factories, for commercial firms, and Government Offices is being arranged. An A.R.P. school has been opened in Calcutta.

August 1942

Women's War Work in India

by

The Marchioness of Linlithgow, C.I.

THE development of women's work in India since the declaration of war was necessarily slow because of the difficulty of persuading the people of India that there was a war, and because of their conviction that, whatever happened elsewhere, India was outside the zone of conflict. From the first moment, however, there was no lack of response to the call for hospital requirements and for comforts for the troops, and the amount turned out by the work-parties all over the country has been and still is colossal. When with typical treachery and ruthlessness the peace of Pearl Harbour was rudely shattered the women of India awoke to the danger which threatened their very existence, and from that moment there has been a most encouraging movement to join the various women's services—the Women's Auxiliary Corps, the Auxiliary Nursing Service, and the Women's Voluntary Service. The difficulties of starting a women's corps in India can only be understood by those who know the country and the people. The vast spaces which have to be covered, the various customs and conditions which exist in different Provinces and States, the modifications which have to be made to meet these conditions, all retard the work which one wishes to accomplish. There have been many complaints on both sides (by those who do the training and by those who are being trained), but, taking it all in all, I think we can look upon the result as gratifying, especially the fact that so many Indian women have come forward. The work which they are called upon to do is alien to anything which they have hitherto undertaken, and my hope is that after the war women will realize what a great need there is for their services and how much can be accomplished by them.

The Director-General Indian Medical Service and I

have done our utmost to popularize the Indian Military Nursing Service, with the object of attracting the better educated type of girl. He has succeeded in raising the status of the Service so that it is now practically on the same footing as the Queen Alexandra Imperial Military Nursing Service. It can no longer be looked upon as inferior, and will, I hope, go from strength to strength even after the war. Over a thousand auxiliary nurses were trained during the first six months after the inauguration of the scheme, and applications continue to pour in. In their zeal to serve many Indian girls apply who are not up to the necessary standard of education, and they have reluctantly to be turned down. The Women's Auxiliary Corps is still in its infancy, but promises well. This force is, of course, under military discipline, and applicants have to sign on for *the duration of the war*, which has the effect of discouraging those who either have or think they have domestic ties. The W.V.S., which started in a few Provinces two years ago, has now spread over most of the country and finds new avenues of service almost daily. At the request of the Home and Defence departments the W.V.S. have now undertaken to deal with all matters pertaining to evacuees, war widows, and abandoned wives— a tremendous task in addition to their many other activities. Occupational therapy has become the cynosure of all eyes and is being pressed forward by all authorities. The W.V.S. has accepted this form of service as one very much within its scope and one which has a vast human interest, and proposes to ask its members to present themselves for training in any one of the many forms which this service to patients can take, from the simplest to the most elaborate. Very interesting facts were given as to the enormous benefit, both mental and physical, derived by the patient who has learned to while away many a weary hour in this way. Indian ladies have been asked to organize this work, for which they are especially well suited, being naturally clever with their fingers.

Finally I should like to say a word about my Silver Trinket Fund. Miss Hope Clark, whose name is so well known in Britain as founder of the Silver Thimble Fund, wrote to me and asked whether I could organize one of the same kind in India. I established it and called it the Silver Trinket Fund and issued my appeal to the women of India. I did not ask for money, although naturally I had many donations from those who had no trinkets to give. It represents gifts from rich and poor, and for many it was a real sacrifice. It often happens that their silver ornaments represent their sole capital, but they all gave willingly, and I have had many touching letters accompanying the gifts. The total of this Fund now stands at eight lakhs, of which nearly seven lakhs has been expended as follows: blood-drying and transfusion plants, bacteriological units, mobile canteens, motor ambulances, mobile hospitals for bombed areas in Britain, motor-buses for convalescent troops, station wagons for Y.W.C.A. war service, donations towards hostels, and finally £10,000 for the provision of an Indian Ward in the Seamen's Hospital at Greenwich. Ambulances, canteens, and all vehicles bear the name of Provinces and States or simply " Women of India." In this way the thoughts of their womenfolk in India are carried to every land where Indian and British soldiers are fighting side by side to crush the evil which overshadows the world, and to put in its place good-fellowship and understanding between all nations.

Doreen Linlithgow

October 1942

As Gold in the Furnace

by

Sir Cyril Atkinson
A Justice of the High Court of Justice

MY excuse for my subject matter is that I was asked to write a *sursum corda* for this book. I have tried with—I am fully conscious of it—but little success. Casting about for a theme, the same words kept forcing themselves to the front, " As gold in the furnace hath He tried them." It seemed to me that they might explain what many truly Christian people find it very hard to understand, but that at any rate they were true, and that they had never been so true since they were written between two and three thousand years ago, because they had never been true at one and the same time of every nation and every individual in the world. Even nations not actually at war are being put to the test; they all have to make up their minds whether boldly to declare that they stand for that which is right, or whether in craven fear they give their aid to that which is evil.

Personally I like the idea. The Anglo-Saxon race, the British nation, I myself, are being tried in the furnace. You see, there are other words adjoining, equally pregnant, " for God proved them and found them worthy for Himself." Here is an incredible force of evil and bestial cruelty striving to destroy every gift of God, everything which we associate with goodness — love, peace, liberty, homes, mothers, little children. It must be the wish of God that goodness shall triumph over this evil thing, but triumph of itself, by reason of the strength within it. There would be no triumph for goodness, no testing in the furnace, if God chose of Himself to destroy this evil. But faith in Him and His promises is part of Christian goodness, and His help, if deserved, and asked in faith, is a weapon available for goodness, and properly to be counted on. But a nation is only the sum total of many individuals; its worth, its goodness, are only the addition of that of its individuals. To them we must turn to increase a nation's strength. All experience shows that individuality is heightened by surrender to something greater than itself, when absorbed in devotion to some transcendent service, a service which may demand the extremity of sacrifice. The transcendent service is there for all to see, demanding of each in his own sphere the surrender, the forgetfulness, of self; only so will a man pass through the ordeal by fire and be found worthy.

Most individuals, even the most unlikely, are capable of rising to unsuspected heights, but many there be who need guides to show the way, O ye Leaders, temporal and spiritual! As gold in the furnace is each and every one of us being tried. Of which of us will it be truly said, " He proved him and found him worthy for Himself " ?

Cyril Atkinson

Part II

ANTHOLOGY—
MAINLY ABOUT INDIA

*

Those who Desired to Live

by

Lascelles Abercrombie

THESE, who desired to live, went out to death;
Dark underground their golden youth is lying;
We live: and there is brightness in our breath
They could not know—the splendour of their dying.

Lascelles Abercrombie

[contributed by PERCY WITHERS]

The Third Visitor

by

J. Redwood Anderson

NOW the last glory of the Angelic flight
had left more dark the winter night;
the last Hozanna of faint choirs on high,
a deeper silence in the sky.

The Wise Men from the East had come and gone
back to the ancient frontiers of the dawn,
leaving their gifts: gold, frankincense, and myrrh;
the Shepherds, too, with simple hearts and pure,
had gone their way, to where their flocks, secure,
slept in an Angel's care.

Now all was still. The lantern-spark
showed where the Child lay fast asleep,
and where, in weary slumbers deep,
his Mother lay beside him: Joseph kept
steadfast vigil while they slept:
and all around
the soft, continual sound
of cattle breathing in the quiet dark.

Then, drawing near along the street,
came, on the night, the measured tread of feet;
the door swung wide: and in the doorway stood
a Warrior, head to heel
clad in completest steel,
and in his hand a drawn sword wet with blood.

The Child cried out: alarmed, the Mother woke.
The Child cried out—and loud through all the skies
that cry re-echoed, and all the deeps of Hell;
as, drawing near, the Warrior fell

down on his knees, and, with stern eyes
fixed on the Child's face, spoke:

" Not gold, nor myrrh, nor frankincense,
nor simple heart of innocence,
my bitter gift I bring
to thee, belovèd King!
For, great as is thy joy in these,
so great thy need of this, if thou wouldst found
on earth, and wouldst maintain,
the blessèd Kingdom of thy Peace."

Thereat he took his sword and laid
it gently on the ground,
and rose, and passed into the night again.

The Child had ceased to cry,
Joseph stood speechless by;
but Mary, sore afraid,
stared at her Son—then bowed her head
meekly: " Thy will be done! " she said,
while from her eyes hot tears of pain
fell like rain
upon the naked blade.

Christmas 1942

J. Redwood Anderson

The Indian Sapper

by

Captain P. S. Bhagat, v.c.

I HAVE the honour of serving in the Royal Bombay
Sappers and Miners. This group is composed of Indians
recruited from the Punjab and the Deccan. Thus it is
composed of people who come from about one-third of
India. They are Mohammedans and Sikhs from Punjab
and Hindus (Mahrattas) from Deccan.

This group had served on all the fronts in the last war
and had won many distinctions. In this war units of the
group are serving with magnificent zeal on all the fronts.
I had the honour of serving with a company of Royal
Bombay Sappers and Miners in Sudan, Eritrea, and
Abyssinia in 1940–41.

Never have I known the Sappers come out of an engagement where they have let down the other branches of the
Army. In fact, far from letting them down, they have done
unbelievable work. They have worked incessantly from
two to three days repairing a road block and making a
track under heavy fire, as in Keren. In this battle the
men from this group, together with the other Sappers,
first made a track up a precipitous hill to enable the
infantry to get supplies. They worked continuously under
observation and fire of the enemy. Having finished this
arduous job, they were then put on the Keren road block
which was obstructing our advance. This major demoli-
tion the Sappers repaired under heavy fire in forty-eight
hours. This piece of work by the Sappers has had the
appreciation of all ranks, including our Commander-in-
Chief, Middle East.

Not only have the Sappers stuck to making tracks and
repairing demolitions, but they have had to lead the advance, clearing mine-fields and obstacles. In one advance
into Abyssinia one party of Sappers worked three days

A Madrassi Signalman of the Indian Signal Corps, from Madura

A Sepoy of the Maratha Light Infantry, from Belgaum, Western India

A Sikh of the Punjab Regiment, from Patiala State

CAPTAIN P. S. BHAGAT, OF THE CORPS OF INDIAN ENGINEERS, THE FIRST
INDIAN V.C. OF THE PRESENT WAR

INDIAN SOLDIERS OF THE RAJPUTANA RIFLES CLEARING RUINS AFTER A
BATTLE IN CYRENAICA

without rest, clearing mine-fields. They were doing this under air attacks and surprise enemy ground attacks. In spite of this, after three days, they were as keen as ever to go on.

Many a daring story can be written about the Indian Sapper, but it is best that the noble record should come out after the conclusion of this war.

Salute to India

by

Gordon Bottomley

KASHMIR and Oudh, Agra and Ajanta;
Anuradhapura, Brindaban, Bijapur;
Akbar, Asoka; Shiva and Siddhartha;
Vishnu and Krishna; Radha and her Gopis—
These were words of power to a dreaming child . . .
Jumna and Parbati; Indus; Brahmaputra;
And other names of water; Karakoram,
Pamir, Kounloun; and other names of snow.
These were words of significance, charming the air,
By their sound creating spiritual sights.
They promised a fairer earth, a finer life
And better purposes than the pursuits
Of ordinary days.

Yet they are of this earth, this life, this purpose
Which life imposes on us. They have come near:
They speak to us of our own duty and theirs.
We have a part in them; and they in us.
They speak of Aryans who found a home
And came to their height among those rivers and
        heights—
Ignorant that any barbarian tribe,
As yet unborn, should foul the Aryan name.
After those Aryans came beneficent Greeks,
Transient in ephemeral, famous arms,
Persistent in immovable, ageless thought.
Strangers, taught by Mohammed that God is one,
Brought their bleak honesty. Persian men
Appeared in the North, shewing how reasonable
And cleansing a thing it is to worship fire
That is in the air—and is not; like a spirit.
India mothered them. She made them hers,

54

But read them by a light that was her own,
As Prince Siddhartha was her chosen child,
The Buddha, The Awakened, The Illumined,
Who would seek truth to its end.

We, we on whom is a burden and a hope,
An aspiration, a sacrifice, and a task—
Are we not concentrated again, and again
Fired to the duty and the sacrifice,
When these proud races that are India
Trust us, and stand with us against hard death?

There was a choice. There is an Eastern race
In Nippon that from early time had lived
By a stern rule of honour called Bushido—
Of stainless honour. They have chosen. They stain it now.
Great India has chosen to stand against them.

There are haughty nations in India; their pride
Is in a thousand years of fearlessness
In battle, of steadfastness in adversity;
And India is in arms.
The hope of the world is made more sure in them.
Mother India, let your embattled sons
Teach us your patience now.
When war is past, shew us how to perceive
Their faith in unseen government of mortality,
Which is stronger than ours—and which, by them and us,
Can attain wisdom at last.

Gordon Bottomley.

Christmas in War-time

by

Clemence Dane

DO you remember how Christmas came
before our world went up in flame?
Jumbled, undated, do memories stir
of frankincense, gold, and myrrh?
Do you remember how Christmas was kept
this year and that year ago—
how, in spite of yourself, you slept
while the stockings were filled,
and woke to a strange white light
on ceiling and walls, and the bedclothes coldly bright;
for with luck there was snow?
Do you remember how Christmas began
thirty years ago?

First—
stockings! Then every one ran
from bedroom to bedroom shouting one to the other.
" Merry Christmas! " rang down the passages.
" Merry Christmas! Now don't get chilled! "
" Merry Christmas, Father and Mother! "
Then breakfast and brown-paper packages,
and no one touching porridge or bacon and sausages.
Then a burst
Of bells and bells, that ring and ring—
" Good people all
to prayer we call "—
and so we get ready for church.

" Hark the herald angels " begins as we enter the porch,
or " Come let us adore Him ";
but " Shepherds watch their flocks by night "
is the hymn that the children love.

There's a threepenny-bit in my glove
for the plate.
Then comes the tale of the birthday Child
and the Maid who bore Him,
Mary mild.
There was no room at the inn,
so she laid Him down on the sweet-smelling hay.
There was an ox and an ass—but no, dear, no,
dogs aren't allowed in church even on Christmas day,
but after the second hymn you can go.
Then you're out in the smooth, pure air.
On you tear
past the frosty graves
and home you come in a glow,
to turkey. Pudding-with-sixpences paves
the dulcet road to the almonds, raisins, and dates,
and there's so much talk
that when you go out for the afternoon walk
the sun's going down already, solemn and huge.
Then the tree! The candles stink;
but I hate the subterfuge
of fairy lights on a Christmas tree, don't you?

Then the waits.
" The First Noël "—that's the choir, I expect,
part-singing, very correct;
but the village children bawl—
" Good King Wenceslas looked out,"
and shout
" Merry Christmas all,"
after the first eight lines.
Give them a shilling, do!
Shut the gate after you, please!

Don't go
in for a minute! How the snow shines!
How quiet it is on Christmas night in the snow!
Look at the sky, black as ink
with such stars in it, and such peace.

" Glory to God in the highest,"
on earth such peace!
Oh—!
Do you remember how Christmas came
before the world went up in flame, in flame?

Shall we remember in just the same
bright-coloured jumble
how Christmas came
this year?
Very few turkeys, and dear.
Mistletoe sold by the pound
(while the guns rumble!),
Everything shuts at four,
black-out at five nineteen:
(crash it comes!)
Father's in Egypt. Mother runs a canteen.
The children are sent away
for fear of Herod—to-morrow is Innocents' Day,
Gas mask! Identity card! (You know, those *were* bombs!)
What more
shall we remember of this strange Christmas feast?
What shall we say?
There was no church bell,
for bells meant " danger! danger! "
Unsummoned we went to pray
and sang " The First Noël."
Our Star in the East
was a Véry flare,
and the 'planes were everywhere.
Christ was born in a raid
that year,
wrapped in his Mother's skirt,
and hurried far underground.
There was no manger.
In damp and dirt
the Child was laid,
and heard the trains clang by,
while all about Him the people lie.

Some laugh, some weep,
some snore, some dream, some grieve.

There was more peace in Bethlehem stall,
with only the ox and the ass
the quiet dark to share
and the scented hay.
Here in the welter
feet pass and repass.
Voices chatter and keep,
the weary from their sleep.
Why not, it is Christmas Eve?
Then the Wise Men come
with treasures three,
a song and a jest and a Christmas-tree
for the Mother and Child in the shelter,
for newborn God in the slum.

Shall we remember it all?
Shall we relive it all?
Shall we forgive it all
in a Christmas yet to come?

O Lovely England

1940

by

Walter de la Mare

O LOVELY England, whose ancient peace
    Mars' direst dangers threat,
    Be on the memory of thy past
Thy sure devotion set!
Give still, true freedom to fulfil,
    Thine all, without regret.

Heed, through the troubles that benumb
    Its voices, stilled, yet clear,
Chaunting their deathless songs—too oft
    To ears that would not hear;
Urging thee—solemn, sweet—to meet
    Thy fate unmoved by fear.

All held most dear in danger lies;
    The foe upon thy seas
Summons to causes, else forlorn,
    The children at thy knees:
Oh, that their hearts in days to come
    May dream, unshamed, of these!

Walter de la Mare

MEN OF THE INDIAN AIR FORCE VOLUNTEER RESERVE
Flight-Lieutenant Rup Chand and his crew before starting on a reconnaissance flight

INDIAN TROOPS SETTING BARBED-WIRE ENTANGLEMENTS IN THE DESERT

A Sepoy of the Punjab Regiment, from Rawalpindi

Naik Corporal of the Royal Garhwhal Rifles, from Nepal

Dogra Naik Corporal of the Royal Frontier Force, from Kangra, Punjab

His *pagri* is khaki with a yellow fringe. He has scarlet caste-markings on his forehead.

To the Indians who Died in Africa

by

T. S. Eliot

A MAN'S destination is his own village,
His own fire, and his wife's cooking;
To sit in front of his own door at sunset
And see his grandson and his neighbour's grandson
Play in the dust together.

Scarred but secure, he has many narratives
To repeat at the hour of conversation
(The warm, or the cool hour, according to the climate),
Of foreign men, who fought in foreign places,
Foreign to each other.

A man's destination is not his destiny.
Every country is home to one man
And exile to another. Where a man dies bravely
At one with his destiny, that soil is his.
Let his village remember.

This was not your land, or ours: but a village in the Mid-
    lands
And one in the Five Rivers, may have the same memories.
Let those who go home tell the same story of you:
Of action with a common purpose, action
None the less fruitful if neither you nor I
Know, until the judgment after death,
What is the fruit of action.

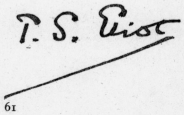

The Shepherd

by

Wilfrid Gibson

WITHIN a wattled cote on Ridgeway Down,
Tending his labouring ewes by the faint light
Of his horn-lantern, through the cloudy night
The shepherd hears high overhead a flight
Of raiders making for some Western town.

Shielding the light within his coat, he stands
For a brief idle moment hearkening
To that deep drone of death upon the wing;
Then turns to his own business, to bring
Innocent life to birth with tender hands.

Wilfrid Gibson.

To an Indian Airman

by

G. Rostrevor Hamilton

HIGH over Europe who dive and turn with
   More than a gannet's grace, what wind
Fans the invisible fire you burn with,
   Guarded, subtle, Indian mind?

Senses alert; yet streaking below you
   Silver Thames unveils a shrine,
Intricate with eyes that show you
   Ganges voyaging divine

Through vast plains that dwarf these meadows,
   Hosts that make our millions small;
Substance, and the drift of shadows;
   Market-clamour; prophet's call.

You, who face with cool derision
   Danger, the air's spinning coin,
You with complex single vision
   Nearly as a mystic join

England, India, one together—
   Thames and Ganges, East and West—
With the same foul storm to weather,
   Worst, that still demands the best.

Best you came to give; we greet you
   Humbly from defended earth,
You in air, where airmen meet you,
   Friend and foe, and know your worth.

George Rostrevor Hamilton

Rabindranath Tagore and his Verse

by

The Rev. W. H. G. Holmes

TO live in Calcutta meant that sooner or later you would come across representatives of almost every Indian race and, indeed, from beyond its frontiers. I was once entertained at a Tibetan tea-party by a Tibetan general who told me that the Oxford Mission was honoured on the mountains of Tibet for what it had done for lads from the northern hills. It meant also this, that there was the opportunity of meeting distinguished Indians from other parts of India. One of the famous men I came across in Calcutta has lately died. His name is known all over the world, and indeed there were few parts of the world he did not visit, but his fame was the fame of a poet, the first Oriental to be awarded the Nobel Prize—Rabindranath Tagore. He invited me to stay with him at Bolpur. On two occasions I did so, and it was in his own home that he used to talk freely to me.

He was the creator of a new form of literary language in Bengal. Before he began to write the literary mode of expression was in ponderous Sanskritic many-syllabled words. To write as one spoke, simply and directly, was literary sacrilege. He, however, would use any word, whatever might be its origin, if it helped to express his thought. It is difficult in these days to realize the intensity of indignation in Bengal which was aroused in " literary " circles by such outrageous violations of all the canons of classical propriety. It is said that in vernacular papers set by University examiners passages from Tagore's writings would be given, with the injunction, " Correct the above." Furiously antagonistic parties arose; there were those who approved and followed; there were those who vilified and rejected. They used most abusive Sanskritic and non-Sanskritic language of one another. No moral infamy could have evoked stronger terms of condemnation; indeed such literary misconduct was regarded as moral infamy. But one thing the opponents could not do; they could not stop the young folk all over Bengal singing Tagore's songs, and learning to love Tagore's simple, luminous prose. He told me quite frankly that he had begun to write songs for students because he wanted to give them something clean and wholesome to sing. He was content with an audience of one, and after dinner he would sing to me song after song in a sweet light tenor, accompanying himself on the tiny little instrument like a doll's harmonium, such as is commonly used in India.

That bitter controversy in his earlier days over the merits of his literary style had, curiously enough, hurt his sensitive soul very deeply, and, being very human, when he got the opportunity of hitting back he hit back hard. It was after he had been given the Nobel Prize. India was exultant, and Bengal all over the moon. One Sunday special trains were chartered, and a multitude went out to Bolpur to present to the poet their fervid congratulations and to express their pride in their famous fellow-countryman. A distinguished Judge of the High Court read an address, and then the Nobel Prize man replied. " It was in very beautiful language," said my informant who heard it, " but he began asking them why they had come. And he told them that they had only come because the Western world had done him honour, and that before that had happened many of them had simply abused him."

Though I would never bind myself to take Bolpur boys into the Oxford Mission Hostel, I had several of them under my care. One of them told me that when the poet was writing the poems of Gitanjali, the collection which first brought his name before the Western world, he often saw him with a New Testament, intently studying the Gospels. It would be a New Testament in English, for he had but the poorest opinion of the Bengali translations of the Bible and the Prayer Book.

Rabindranath Tagore does not seem to have been drawn to Christianity in the sense that he ever felt the possibility of becoming a member of Christ's Church, but it is difficult to read Gitanjali without feeling that his whole conception of God and the possibility of our intimacy with Him was what he had found in his meditations on the Gospels.

Here is Thy footstool and there rest Thy feet where live the poorest and the lowliest and the lost. When I try to bow to Thee, my obeisance cannot reach down to the depth where Thy feet rest among the poorest and lowliest and lost. Pride can never approach to where Thou walkest in the clothes of the humble among the poorest and lowliest and lost. My heart can never find its way to where Thou keepest company among the poorest, the lowliest, and the lost.

Thou keepest company with the companionless among the poorest, the lowliest, and the lost.

Again:

He is there where the tiller is tilling the hard ground and where the pathmaker is making stones. . . . He is with them in sun and in shower, and his garment is covered with dust. . . . Deliverance? Where is this deliverance to be found? Our Master Himself has joyfully taken upon Him the bonds of creation; He is bound with us all for ever.

You came down from Your throne and stood at my cottage door.

There is also an echo of the gracious invitation, " Come unto Me." It is given to the foolish ones who try to " carry themselves upon their own shoulders," who " go and beg at their own doors ":

Leave all thy burdens on His hands Who can bear all.

There is another echo, this time of the words, " There standeth one among you Whom ye know not " (St John i, 26):

They push Thee and pass Thee on the dusty road, taking Thee for naught.

The steps that I have heard are the same that are echoing from star to star.

Have you not heard His silent steps? He comes, ever comes. . . . In sorrow after sorrow it is His steps that press upon my heart, and it is the golden touch of His feet that makes my joy to shine.

There is the sudden coming of the Divine King for whom no preparation has been made, surely an echo of the Parable of the Virgins:

> The voice came " Wake up! Delay not! . . . The King has come—but where are lights, where are wreaths? Where is the throne to seat Him? Oh, shame, oh, utter shame! "

There is an echo of the story of the Samaritan woman at the well:

> I heard not Thy steps as Thou camest. Thine eyes were sad when they fell on me; Thy voice was tired as Thou spokest low —" Ah, I am a thirsty traveller." I started up from my daydreams and poured water from my jar on Thy joined palms. . . . What had I done for Thee to keep me in remembrance? But the memory that I could give water to Thee to allay Thy thirst will cling to my heart and enfold it in sweetness.

And finally, " Thou art the Brother amongst my brothers " recalls the injunction, " Go to My brethren " (St John xx, 17), and the glad assurance, " He is not ashamed to call them brethren " (Hebrews ii, 11).

He could think clearly as well as sing sweetly. So when the war came Tagore went straight as a die; he saw clearly, and he spoke clearly. Here are his words:

> The conscience of the world has been profoundly shocked at the latest manifestation of the arrogant unrighteousness of the present rulers of Germany; this is but the culmination of a long series of intimidations of the weak, from the suppression of the Jewish people in the Reich to the rape of that gallant and truly liberal state of Czecho-Slovakia. Our voice may not perhaps reach the ears of the faction in power in Germany, for it is not borne on wings of high-explosive shells; I can only hope that humanity may emerge triumphant, and that the decencies of life and freedom for the oppressed peoples may be firmly established for all time in a world purified through this terrible bath of blood.

W. H. G. Holmes

Vae Victori

by

P. H. B. Lyon, M.C.
Headmaster of Rugby

AT your decree we die or live,
 Our goods are yours to burn or bind;
 Our honour, which we would not give,
You cannot take—Ah! fools and blind,

What conquest wins you innocence,
What mastery a heart unstained?
Your own drawn sword shall drive you hence
When this red moon of war has waned.

What though your ships should ride the seas
Your armies sweep from tide to tide?
Man lives by higher things than these;
You shall go back unsatisfied.

And not to-morrow or to-day
The scales are set, the balance told;
They still have judgment who betray
Their Christ for glory or for gold.

The fruits of victory are sweet.
Ride on to reap your just reward!
Ride on in arrogance, to meet
The angel with the flaming sword!

Hugh Lyon

The Secret of France

by

Sir John Pollock

MANY French people as yet barely middle-aged remember the delighted excitement caused during the last war by the arrival in France of our Indian troops; how, at Toulouse for instance, crowds flocked to their trains in the station with gifts of fruit and flowers; how warm was the admiration of their gallant bearing, their frank expression, their perfect discipline, their beautiful coloured silken shirts.

While France and its Government were with us in this war, as the Free France of General de Gaulle is happily still with us, there was less opportunity for such manifestations. Yet there were Indians with the British Expeditionary Force in France, and some, saved from Dunkirk, related how graciously the women of France welcomed them as they marched through town and village. " The *Memsahibs*," said one of them, " danced for us and gave us flowers."

This picture of French popular manners will astonish no one who knows France. . . .

For every man and every woman France—the France that was and yet shall be again—has her secret meaning. To some she spells the exhilarating beauty of the South—of Provence, Languedoc, and the Côte d'Azur, that the French combine in one alluring word, " le Midi "; to others, holidays spent in quiet enjoyment of a delicious climate, perfect cookery, wine that makes Bacchus a reality, or holidays, if you prefer these, spent in the factitious excitements of the City of Light; to yet others, women all, the marvellous ' line ' achieved by French dressmakers; and again, the patient, often noble, work of scholars and scientists, the Renans, Pasteurs, Bédiers, Curies, or the music of Offenbach, Debussy, Bizet, Saint-Saëns, or the plays of a hundred brilliant authors. I speak of the moderns alone.

The diversity of France's mind is as great as that of her natural resources. But throughout it run the twin threads that perhaps more than anything give the tone to all that we know as French, whether in the study or in the kitchen or in the theatre or the concert hall, or even in the world of field and sunshine: a sort of fierce idealism, and a joy in perfect execution. How far the French character affects or is affected by the varied beauty of French landscape may be a question; let us note that the most famous views and those less known but not less lovely almost all owe something to the hand of man. There is a bridge spanning that slow river or rushing stream; a ruined castle dominating this gorge; in the most unexpected place a hamlet clinging to a crag, a farm half hidden in the valley, a forester's hut revealed in its sudden clearing. The very trees planted by Napoleon along the grand high roads of France charge the landscape with a touch of human genius.

A Frenchman seldom does anything without having in his mind an image of what he wants to do. Hardly a Frenchman but wants to do what he does in the best way possible. That image keeps his ideal ever fresh; that yearning towards the best gives his hand that delicacy that in most countries belongs to the artist alone. Hence the individual touch visible in the work of even the humblest French artisan; hence too the fact that in France innumerable artisans and craftsmen persist despite modern mass production, and even tinge French mass production with the spirit of their talent. To take two examples from very commonplace achievement: nowhere is motor-car carriage-work, mass production indeed, so neat, so handsome, so comfortable as is the French; nor can the preparation and packing of proprietary drugs in any country compare with those made up in France.

Doubtless this comes to the same as saying that in every Frenchman is something of an artist. And herein must be the secret of the fact, often noted, that in France the artist is accounted more highly than elsewhere in Europe. The thinker too; but in France the thinker is keenly judged by his power of exposition, so that Frenchmen of science from Descartes downward have attained a clarity in the transmission of their thoughts that is in itself evidence of the artist's share in their minds. For it is certain that the French nation as a whole reverences men who put aside calculation of worldly success in order to pursue work imposed on them by the spirit. In England a writer, painter, musician, or actor is thought a queer fish; it was a well-known American novelist who said, " I don't mind being treated like an inferior, but I do object to being talked to as a woman." In France the artist is treated with instant respect and admiration even by the generality. In France things of the mind count before things of the body. Even in these lower delights it is quality not quantity that counts with the French. Good taste is their rule and the grace that saves them, nine times out of ten, from vulgarity even amid vulgar surroundings. That is the legacy of long tradition in France, consolidated and extended to influence the whole world by the system developed during the long reign of Louis XIV, to whom Frenchmen themselves often underestimate their debt. An ideal design present in the mind: execution of the design as nearly perfect as it can be made. Like the artists of ancient Athens, the French work not only for themselves but for the gods. Therein lies the real secret of France. That example is the gift of France to the world, and therefore must we pray in this year of grace that it may be the last of France's desolation under the tyranny of barbarian invasion. For the spirit of France is the spirit of civilization.

John Pollock

A Sepoy Looks at the War

by

" Rasp "

MY old Indian Army friend, Havildar Sher Khan, has just been to thank me for arranging for him to visit one of our big munition factories.

I had met Sher Khan wandering rather aimlessly in the town—happy to have come to Britain to fight, but hard put to it to find amusement. Where could he find anything like the narrow, smelly, friendly bazaar with its tiny lights and Indian cinemas? He must miss even the beggar and his bowl. He certainly misses the sickly sweetmeats, hot from the sizzling fat, the loud-voiced friendly haggling in his own language for the cheap mirror and gay handkerchief.

All day he must wear the stiff *patloons* (trousers), for in England one cannot sit in the street and haggle in comfortable *dhoti* (loin-cloth). All day the heavy boots must tramp the hard pavements, so that he never knows the ease of sandals paddling along through the soft dust at the roadside.

I could not provide his heart's longing, but I could arrange for him and twenty friends to see over one of our great munition works. Here is his tale of what he saw.

" Sahib," he said, " by your great kindness I have seen a wonderful sight. The *Burra* Sahib [Superintendent] himself met us at the gate, and all the police fell back as he appeared and quickly allowed us to pass in.

" He divided us in small parties, each with an N.C.O. who spoke *Angrezi*,[1] and told us that eleven months ago this site had been green fields with grazing sheep. Yet within six months the factory had produced the first gun, and within seven months twenty-five guns per month.

[1] English.

72

When he told me what it produces now a month he named a figure which made me gasp.

"To-day, too, instead of hedges we saw well-concealed defences, deep as our company defence schemes are in depth, and A.A. defences which the workers in the Home Guard can themselves man in a few seconds. Inside the defences were wide roads, huge camouflaged sheds of steel and concrete, and green lawns and even flower-beds.

"Outside one shed was a puzzling sight—a group of mem-sahibs [ladies] not only wearing trousers, but, strangest of all, wearing coloured *safas* [turbans]. The Superintendent told us that they made the heavy guns—at which we laughed heartily, for they were little women, and, as you well know, in India not all men can do such work, but only *Mistris* [literally, clever men], and our women just make our bread.

"It is only in certain castes in India that women wear trousers, so we asked to what castes these belonged, but they could not understand this question. Then, too, we noticed that they wore their overalls, like our shirts, outside their trousers. This is wisdom, for, as in India, it is cooling and free.

"We entered the first big shed and saw that the Superintendent had not been joking, for there, making the guns, were a few men and hundreds of women, each one working on a machine as big as a bullock-cart, shafts and all.

"These mems were the ones with green *safas*, while those with red were like N.C.O.'s, in charge of perhaps half a dozen machines. One very small mem with a blue *safa* lifted the guns—bigger than elephants' trunks—with her little finger."

Here I felt that Sher Khan's imagination was getting the better of him and pressed for details.

"She was up in the roof in a thing which looked like a footbridge over a railway; and from this hung a chain with grappling-hooks. These gripped the gun, and then the mem pressed her finger, and up it rose and was carried to the next bay in the building, where she handed it to the next worker. Each mem did one job.

" One machine bored with sharp teeth through the rough steel barrel, which was then lifted to the next machine, which carved and polished the outside. The next polished the inside of the bore till it shone, smooth as silk ; the next cut the rifling, and so on till the barrel was complete.

" We too, were asked many questions, such as, if we did not find it very cold here. But why should we? We Punjabis are used to the snows and bitter winds of the Punjab hills.

" As we passed on we saw extractors and breech blocks being planed, the hard steel curling off as easily as the wood from the carpenter's plane at home. Other mems did the fitting, placing an instrument inside which marked with blue those parts which must be filed away, and these they filed as easily as the shoeing-smith rasps a hoof. Then their inspector, a mem with a white *safa*, checked the measurements with a delicate instrument and an eye-piece.

" There is nothing these mems cannot do. One told us that she had been a hairdresser till a few months ago ; another had been in a bioscope [cinema] ; and a third said she had just been married. But I think she was joking, for she was old, at least thirty, and, as all the world knows, sixteen is the age for marriage. Besides, how could she bake her man's bread?

" Then they took us to the canteen and offered us tea, but we explained that it is the time of the Ramzan [a period of religious fasting], and that we keep the Roza [days of fasting] till the new moon appears. They were sad to find we could not take even water or cigarettes.

" They seemed surprised to hear that our principal food is *chapatties*, vegetables, and *dhall* [lentils], with very little meat, preferably goat, and were still more surprised to hear that the Government could give us not only all the spices we need, like ginger, garlic, chillies, and so on, but lots of onions.

" I don't speak English, but I understood one mem who, laughing, held out her hand and said, ' Oh, onions, please.'

" Then they took us to the last bay, where all the parts we had seen were assembled, and after they had been passed

74

by the chief inspector we were allowed to load, test, and fire.

"Here they were overjoyed, because they had just received news from London that they had the biggest production record in all England for last month. Yet here a year ago sheep grazed. Truly it is a marvel. And so we left.

"Sahib, in India we know that you men do many things, and your mems make you comfortable homes and keep you well, but will not gather even the tennis balls. Yet I, who have come six thousand miles, now know that they can quickly learn to do things undreamed of in India and make the very guns men need."

"Well," said I, "you'll have a grand tale to tell in India."

"This," said Sher Khan, "is a very sad thing I have to say. I may never tell it to my wife—she would never believe me. It is beyond understanding."

Rash.

To India

by

The Countess Roberts of Kandahar, D.B.E.

RUDYARD KIPLING once gave praise to Allah, who had given him two separate sides to his head, and told how the gift brought with it an insight into the hearts and minds of other races than his own. Few who, like him, were born in India can claim to have been so greatly gifted, but perhaps it is not too much to hope that the land which gave them birth, whether in the great plains, like my father, or, like myself, among the deodars of Himalaya, bred in them a wish to understand and a sympathy for her peoples which, like all good gifts, have added greatly to the fullness of life.

Service in a country has also its boons to bestow on those who serve her, and my father's long years in India, " the wonderful land of my adoption," brought him many a valued friendship. Rulers of States, landowners, stalwart men of the frontier, soldiers, and sportsmen, he reckoned among his friends; he gloried in the soldierly qualities of the Indian Army and in the comradeship which exists between the British officers and their men. In the last year of his life nothing gave him greater pleasure than his appointment by the King to be Colonel-in-Chief of the force which left the shores of India to take its part in the Great War, and he went with affection in his heart to greet them when they came to France.

In the years that followed the men of India volunteered in large numbers. It is written that in one small village in the Punjab four hundred and sixty men were recruited from a male population of less than nine hundred. One wonders if that record can be matched by any village in the far-flung dominions of the King!

Now, in these days, the armies of India are afoot once more. In the years that have passed since they last came over the sea the methods of warfare have greatly changed. But the sons of the men who fought in 1914–18, the descendants of those who earned fame among the Afghan hills and in many a hard struggle on the frontier, of the men of the Guides who, in the heat of an Indian summer, marched close on nine hundred miles in twenty-two days to the siege of Delhi, the horsemen, heirs of the men to whom through the ages of India's history war has meant a horse and saddle, a spear and a sword, whose forefathers, maybe, " rode with Nawab Amir Khan in the old Maratta War," one and all, on land and sea, and in the strange new element of the air, have adapted themselves to the new conditions as readily as their British comrades and the men from the distant dominions; have fought well, and have added fresh laurels to a splendid story.

In many a village the women of India wait for news of their men; may they learn that the needs of their husbands and sons are not forgotten, and that ' comforts ' of all kinds are being sent to them in generous quantity.

Robert.

Dr Watson's Christian Name

A Brief Contribution to the Exegetical Literature of Sherlock Holmes

by

Dorothy L. Sayers

IT has always been a matter of astonishment to Dr Watson's friends, and perhaps of a little malicious amusement to his detractors, to observe that his wife [1] apparently did not know her own husband's name. There can be no possible doubt that Watson's first Christian name was John. The name " John H. Watson " appears, conspicuously and in capital letters, on the title-page of *A Study in Scarlet*,[2] and it is not for one moment to be supposed that Watson, proudly contemplating the proofs of his first literary venture, would have allowed it to go forth into the world under a name that was not his. Yet in 1891 we find Watson publishing the story of " The Man with the Twisted Lip," in the course of which Mrs Watson addresses him as " James."

Mr H. W. Bell (*Sherlock Holmes and Dr Watson*, p. 66, n. 2) has been unable to account for this, and despairingly suggests that it is a mere printer's error. " Watson," he remarks, with much truth, " was a very careless reader of proof." But if he had read the proofs *at all* this particular error could not have failed to catch his eye. A man's own name is a subject on which he is sensitive; nothing is more exasperating than to be ' called out of one's name.' Moreover, in December 1891 Mary Watson was still alive. Tenderly devoted as she was to her husband, she could not have failed to read his stories attentively on publication

[1] His first wife, and only true love, Mary, *née* Morstan. There is a conspiracy afoot to provide Watson with as many wives as Henry VIII, but, however this may be, only one is ever mentioned by him and only one left any abiding memory in his heart.

[2] It also appears, plainly marked in capitals, at the foot of the sketch-plan illustrating *The Priory School*.

in the *Strand Magazine*, and she would have undoubtedly drawn his attention to an error so ridiculous and immediately reflecting on herself. In the month immediately preceding the Doctor had made another trivial slip in connexion with his wife's affairs; he said that during the period of the adventure of " *The Five Orange Pips* " Mrs Watson was visiting her mother. Mrs Watson, who was, of course, an orphan (*Sign of Four*), evidently took pains to point out this error and see that the careless author made a note of it; for on the publication of the collected *Adventures* in 1892 the word " mother " is duly corrected to " aunt." [1] On such dull matters as dates and historical facts the dear woman would offer no comment, but on any detail affecting her domestic life she would pounce like a tigress. Yet the name " James " was left unaltered in all succeeding editions of the story.

How are we to explain this?

The solution is probably to be sought in a direction which has been too little explored by the commentators. In fact, the whole subject of Dr Watson's second Christian name has been treated with a levity and carelessness which are a positive disgrace to scholarship.

Mr S. C. Roberts (*Dr Watson*, p. 9) suggests, without an atom of evidence, that Watson's mother was " a devout woman with Tractarian leanings," merely in order to presume that her son was named " John Henry " after the great Newman himself. If there were, in Dr Watson's character, the slightest trace of Tractarian sympathies, or even of strong anti-Tractarian sympathies, the suggestion might carry some weight, for no one could be brought up in an atmosphere of Tractarian fervour without reacting to it in one way or another. But Watson's religious views remain completely colourless. Of Holmes's beliefs we know little, but of Dr Watson's, nothing. The hypothesis is purely frivolous.

---

[1] It appears from this that Watson, with a shyness not uncommon in authors, did not show his wife either his manuscript or his proofs. After publication he would probably leave the *Strand* carelessly lying about the house to be dutifully perused by Mary, to his deprecatory astonishment.

Mr H. W. Bell, with his wonted scholarly caution, rejects the Newman theory. " It must be objected," he says (*Sherlock Holmes and Dr Watson, loc cit.*), " that Newman had become a Catholic in 1845, seven years before the date which Mr Roberts proposes for Watson's birth. If Mrs Watson had indeed had . . . Tractarian leanings . . . she would hardly have named her son after the illustrious convert." But Mr Bell makes no effort to solve the problem himself, although this observation actually forms part of his note about the name James. True solution was staring him in the face, and if he had given the matter proper attention he must have seen it. But he dismissed " James " as a typographical error and went on his way, leaving the Watsons still enveloped in a cloud of ridicule.

Mr T. S. Blakeney behaves still more absurdly. Postulating a composite James-John authorship, he calls for a J. M. Robertson to " sift the accretions of the pseudo-Watson from the core of matter deriving solely from the hand of the veritable John Henry "—forgetting that John *Henry* Watson is even more conjectural than *Jesus* Barabbas,[1] and thus making the fabulous name into a guarantee of the genuine identity. Illogicality could go no further.[2]

There is only one plain conclusion to be drawn from the facts. Only one name will reconcile the appellation James with the initial letter H. The doctor's full name was John Hamish Watson.

Hamish is, of course, the Scottish form of James. There is no reason to feel any surprise that Dr Watson should bear a Scottish name. Sturdily and essentially English as he was, he may well, like most English people, have had a Scottish ancestor in his family tree. The English are probably the only people in the world who actually make

---

[1] For the complicated structure of deduction built by Drews and others upon this highly disputable reading, see Thorburn, *Mythical Interpretation of the Gospels*, p. 264 *sqq.*

[2] It is only justice to add that Mr S. C. Roberts lost no time in pointing out this lamentable confusion between " objective date and legitimate surmise " and deprecating it with equal firmness and courtesy. (*Observer*, October 30, 1932.)

a boast of mongrel ancestry. The words "hundred per cent. English" are never heard on true English lips, for the English know well enough that their cross-breeding is their strength. Scotsmen, Welshmen, Irishmen, Jews, cling to the purity of their descent, realizing that to blend their nationality is to lose it. But English blood is so strong that one drop of it will make the whole blend English. A hundred Scottish ancestors, nay, even a Scottish mother, would in no way affect the indomitable Englishry of Dr Watson.

In fact, there is some slight evidence for a Scots strain in Watson. It may not be mere coincidence that led Holmes (a shrewd student of national character) to select the adjective ' pawky' for the vein of humour which Watson displayed during the adventure of *The Valley of Fear* and which took his distinguished friend a little aback. Watson's mother may have been a Scot—not, I think, a Highland woman, but a native of Eastern Scotland [1]—and it may have pleased her to give a Scottish name to her son.

But there is no real need to assume Scottish descent to explain a Scottish name. The English, with their romantic love of the outlandish, their tendency to concoct a mixed genealogy for themselves, and their incurable disdain for other people's racial sensitiveness, are notorious for their habit of annexing foreign names, merely because they think them pretty or poetical. The suburbs of London swarm with Douglases and Donalds, Malcolms and Ians, whose ancestors never crossed the border, with Patricks and Brians and Sheilas who owe nothing to Erin, with Gwladyses whose names are spelled according to fancy and not to inheritance, and with other exotics still more remote. The combination John Hamish Watson has nothing about it that need disconcert us.

Nor is it at all unusual for a wife to call her husband by his second name, in preference to his first. It is a pretty thought that he should be known to her by a name which is not the common property of the outside world. Possibly

[1] The true Highlander is a Celt—quick-tempered, poetical, and humourless—everything that Watson was not. Dourness and pawkiness belong to the Aberdeen side of the country.

Mrs Watson did not care for the name John. It was painfully connected in her mind with Major John Sholto, who had helped to ruin her father and bring about his death. " Johnnie " would be open to the same objection; besides, no one with any sense of the fitting would call Dr Watson " Johnnie." There seems to be nothing specially objectionable about " Jack," but it may have seemed to her too flippant and jaunty. The probability, however, is that she preferred to cut out all association with " John." There remained the choice between " Hamish " and a pet-name. " Hamish " seemed to her perhaps a little high-falutin. By playfully re-Englishing it to " James " she found for her husband a pet-name which was his own name as well; a name by which no one else would think of calling him, a name free from the tiresome skittishness of the ordinary pet-name, and a name eminently suitable to his solid and sober character.[1]

It would be natural enough that Dr Watson, accustomed for over three years to being called James by his wife, should automatically incorporate the name into his story when reproducing the dialogue between his Mary and himself—forgetting that, to the uninstructed reader, it might present an odd appearance. Nor would Mrs Watson correct it. To her, the doctor was " her James "; that she should be supposed to call him by any other name would seem to her unnatural, almost improper. Smilingly she perused the pages of the *Strand*, delighted to recognize herself and her home life accurately portrayed in all the glory of print.

Dorothy L. Sayers

---

[1] An interesting parallel case of the interchangeability of " James " and " Hamish " occurs in Mrs Wood's novel *The Channings*: " The eldest son of the family, James; or, as he was invariably styled, Hamish." This book was extremely popular in the nineties, achieving its hundred-and-fortieth thousand in 1895, and may actually have suggested the idea to Mrs Watson.

Rabindranath Tagore as Man and Friend : A Personal Tribute

by

J. A. Spender, c.ʜ.

ONE evening sitting by the Taj Mahal, at Agra, I fell into talk with a young Indian who had come, as I had, to drink in the charm of that uniquely beautiful spot. With a little encouragement he poured out his heart in enthusiasm for the " sacred soil of the Indian people." For illustration of one thing that he specially felt he chose that poet and philosopher, Rabindranath Tagore.

He said that in England they judged him by the few poems and essays which he had written in their language or which had been translated into it. These were indeed charming accomplishments, and it was wonderful that he should be able to write as he did in a foreign language, but they gave not the slightest impression of what he was when he wrote in his own language for his own people.

I find a deep and great satisfaction in his English writings. One essay especially, " The Philosophy of our People," seems to me masterly and profound. Nor need he fear comparison with any English writer with regard to his letters in the English language. He was a real letter-writer, serious, intimate, and light of touch. But in the end it is the response of his own people and the immense influence he has had on them for the last fifty years which give the measure of his stature. No Englishman can pretend to judge of this, but I can contribute a memory of the man Tagore which helps me and may help others to understand it.

When I was last in India—unhappily as long ago as 1926 —he asked me and my wife to spend a week with him in his *Asram* at Santiniketan, in Bengal. We went, and came away with an immense respect for him and the work he was doing for India.

He was the most practical of poets. His *Asram* and the neighbouring village of Surrul were educational colonies in which Indian boys and girls were being brought up in the way in which he thought young Indians should walk if they were to play their part in redeeming their country from the poverty and squalor which defaced it. He had his pride about alien rule, and there were tragic incidents which broke down his habitual patience and reserve. " I am wounded in my soul," and so saying he cast away his British knighthood. But this was a passing mood, from which he returned quickly to his habitual charity and reserve, and above all to his steady thought that Indians themselves must be made fit to govern India, and that they must not let anger or bitter memories turn them from that immediate task.

His own part in this was to make his rural centre a model of what others ought to be. He might throw his poetic mantle about it, but there was to be no sentimental vagueness in its work. The organization was to be clear and firm, the education thorough and practical, but without the breach between the utilitarian and the cultural which he saw deepening and widening in Western education. He poured his own fortune into it, but it needed regular support from outside; and he was a most efficient manager and administrator, keen to show that his accounts balanced and that any money given to him was spent to the utmost advantage, not thrown as a sop to the poet and mystic experimenting with the young idea. To keep it going on the scale to which it grew and to provide for its future was a large part of his work in life in his later years. There were friends who said it was too much for him, and that it was drawing him away from his poetry and philosophy, but to all these he answered that it was his work in life, his poetry and philosophy.

As we saw it, Santiniketan was a combination of higher school for boys and girls, agricultural college with its experimental farm and research laboratory, and departments for higher students in philosophy, painting, and music. If you went into the painting-room you saw a lad seated on a low dais singing Bengali folk-songs to his own accompaniment on a beautiful old Indian instrument while a companion wrote them down in musical notation, and a score more went silently on with their painting and drawing. Outside there might be a company of Boy Scouts trained on the English model to go whenever the call to " come and clear up " came from the adjoining villages. They went fearlessly when cholera or plague was reported, and saw that wells were decontaminated, that water was boiled, and that all filth or ordure which might spread infection was swept away.

It was the combination of these things that made Santiniketan unique. The poet presided over it all, and I still see him sitting in the great chair in the open pavilion in the centre of the village, a beautiful benevolent presence in the charming blue robes that fell so gracefully into classical folds. The scene would not bear transplanting to the West. It needs the Indian sun and the Indian atmosphere to make it seem just right and natural that boys and girls should walk in procession up and down avenues of stately trees, singing their morning and evening hymns, and that their classrooms should be green swards under these trees. The Westerner who tries to copy these things is all the time in danger of making them seem artificial. Tagore never left you in doubt that if a poet and mystic he was determined not to let his vision fade into a poet's dream. He saw life as a blend of poetry, art, philosophy, religion, and the daily task, all of which had to be brought together to make the whole man or woman.

J. A. Spender.

Cyrenaica in the Fifth Century

by

Helen Waddell

[THE original of this fragment of translation is in the *Dialogi* of
Sulpicius Severus of Toulouse, written on the eve of the barbarian
invasion, in the year when France was being stripped of the Legions,
for the defence of Italy.

> Naught but the terror of the Roman name
> Defends the open frontier:
> To-night there is no watch upon the Rhine.

Yet there is no more premonition of disaster in the proud security
of Claudian's verse, than in this quiet prose.

With his elder contemporary, Ausonius of Bordeaux, Sulpicius
Severus represents the first achievement in letters of that *haute bour-
geoisie* which has made France the second patria of civilized men; but,
unlike Ausonius, he had abandoned great possessions and a brilliant
career at the bar to follow, in St Jerome's phrase, " naked, the naked
Christ." He came of good stock of Aquitaine, married into a consular
family, and wealth flowed to him from both; but in the springtides of
success he came under the spell of " Martin," as he plainly called him,
ex-soldier of the Legion, and destined, as St Martin of Tours, to rival
even St Denys in the heart, though not the banners, of France. After
that, as Paulinus of Nola once wrote to him, no voice could call him
back " to that easy spacious road. . . . Preferring the preaching of the
fishermen to the prose of Cicero, aye, and your own, you took refuge in
the silence of devotion." Yet a silence not wholly unbroken. Though
only a few pages remain, there is enough to show the first clear spring
of Gallic prose, subtle, ironic, and humane.]

WE had arranged to meet, my friend Gallus and
I: he is very dear to me, not only for his own
quality, but for the sake of Martin's memory:
he had been his disciple, as I was. And as we talked who
should come upon us but my friend Postumianus back
from the East, whither he had gone from his own country
three years ago. I held him, this man so dear to me, in my
arms. We stood gazing at each other, blockishly, and wept
for very joy, and gazed again, walking and stopping, till
at last we flung our cloaks upon the ground and sat down
together. Postumianus fixed his eyes on me: he was the
first to speak.

" I was in Egypt," he said, " in the interior, when the
humour took me that I would make my way to the sea.
As it happened, there was a merchant ship in harbour,
loading up with cargo for Narbonne. That night I dreamt
I saw you standing by me, and you laid your hand on me
as though you would draw me to get on board the ship.
Soon after the day broke; I sat up in the place where I
had been lying; and, as I went back over my dream in my
own mind, I was seized of a sudden with such a longing for
you that I stayed for nothing and went straight on board.
A month later we touched at Marseilles: another ten days
brought me here: a fair voyage answering a faithful purpose. And now do *you* talk, for whom I have crossed so
many lands and sailed so many seas, to touch your hand
and have your company, and all the world away."

" For my part," said I, " my mind and my soul were
with you all the while you were in Egypt. . . . You will
not take it ill that your friend Gallus is here, who, as you
see, is beaming with pleasure at your coming, even as I am."

" Indeed," said Postumianus, " I shall be glad of his
company, for though I have small acquaintance with him,
any man that is so dear to you cannot but be dear to me,
above all when he was one of Martin's men. I promise
you it will be no trouble to me to talk. I am here for nothing
else but to unload my wordy self on my old Sulpicius," and
he caught me by both hands.

" Then," said I, " tell us the whole story of your pil-
grimage: how the faith of Christ fares in the East: what
quiet may be there for holy men: for indeed in these parts
where now we live life has become a weariness, and we
would fain know if even in the desert there is room to live
as Christian men."

" That will I do," said Postumianus; and, moving the
cloak on which he sat a little nearer me, he began to speak.

" It is three years, Sulpicius, since I said good-bye to you
and left this place. We weighed anchor at Narbonne: five
days at sea brought us to the port of Africa, so prosperous,
by God's grace, was our voyage. I had the satisfaction of
seeing Carthage and visiting the holy places: and above

all, I knelt before the grave of Cyprian the Martyr. A fortnight later I was back again in the port, and we made for the open sea. Our course was set for Alexandria, but a southerly wind fought us back, and would have had us on the sand-banks at Syrte, only that our wary seamen dropped anchor and let the ship ride. Before our eyes stretched the unbroken line of coast; we set out in skiffs, and, stepping ashore, we looked on a country empty of any trace of human toil or habitation. There is a singular pleasure in exploring new places: and in the zest of it I went some way farther. About a mile or so from the beach I spy a little hut amid the sands, its roof like the keel of a ship, coming close down to the ground, and pretty strongly morticed: not that there is any cause to fear a downpour of rain (for, indeed, a shower in those parts is a thing unheard of), but that the force of the wind is such that in the balmiest weather let but a breath of wind begin to blow and the wreckage on land is worse than on any sea. No green thing burgeons here, no standing corn, in this unquiet earth, these thirsty sands shifting at every stirring of the wind. At one spot, indeed, where certain headlands rise from the sea and break the force of the winds, the soil is something more stable, and bears a scant harsh grass: it makes a tolerable pasture for the sheep. The inhabitants live on milk: the better managers among them, or, if you like, the wealthier, eat barley bread. This is the only harvest the soil will bear: thanks to the swiftness of its growth in that climate and that soil, it can escape destruction by the wind: between that sowing of the seed and its ripening there are, I am told, but thirty days. Men live in this land for no other reason but this: that here all are free from tribute. It is the ultimate verge of Cyrenaica, neighbour to the desert that lies between Egypt and Africa; and in old time Cato, fleeing from Caesar with his army, passed this way.

" The hut that I had seen was but a spear's cast distant: I made my way towards it and found an old man clad in skins, turning a grindstone with his hand: I greeted him, and he made us benignly welcome. We told him how we had been cast upon this coast, and could not yet take off again, becalmed in the quiet of the sea : that we had come ashore, as is the way of human curiosity, to see what kind of place it was and what manner of men its inhabitants might be : that we were Christians, and above all would seek to know if there were Christian men amid these solitudes.

" Then, indeed, weeping for joy, he cast himself at our feet : again and again he embraced me and then, strewing sheepskins on the ground, would have us sit down, and set before us a truly sumptuous meal, no less than half a loaf of barley bread. There were four of us, himself the fifth. He also brought a bunch of herbs the name of which I have forgotten, bushy in leaf like mint, with a taste like honey, extraordinarily delicate and sweet : we were delighted with it and ate till we could eat no more."

At that, I glanced smiling at my friend Gallus. " Well, Gallus," said I, " what think you of that for a feast, a bunch of herbs and half a loaf among five men ? "

Gallus reddened a little, for he is a sensitive soul, at my teasing. " There you go, Sulpicius," said he. " You never let a chance go by of poking fun at my greed. But it is inhumane of you to force us Gallic men to live as the angels do—though I am myself convinced that the angels eat for the sheer pleasure of eating : and I should think very poorly of that barley loaf even if I had it to my sole self. I'll let your Cyrenian have it, whose necessity or nature it is to go hungry : as for the rest of you, the good tossing you had must have left you too seasick to care. For my part, we are a long way from the sea, and as I have often insisted to you, we are good *Gaulois*, so let my friend get on with the story of his Cyrenian."

" After this," says Postumianus, " I must beware of remarking anybody's abstinence, lest harsh example should annoy these Gauls. I had planned to tell the tale of that Cyrenian feast and the banquets that followed (for we were with our host for a week) : but I pass over it, or Gallus will think I am talking at him. Well, next day, when some of the neighbours began drifting in to see us, we found out what our host had taken great pains to keep from us, that he was a priest. Thereafter we went with him to the church, about a mile away, but shut out of sight from us by the bulk of the mountain. It was thatched with brushwood, not much more ambitious than our host's habitation, where a man could not stand without stooping. When we began inquiring into the way they lived, this moved us above all, that nothing among them is bought or sold. What fraud or theft may be they know not. Gold and silver, which mortal men prize first, they have not, nor desire to have: for when I tried to offer the priest ten gold pieces he shrank away, protesting in his nobler wisdom, 'the Church is not builded by gold but rather destroyed by it.' For affection's sake we urged on him a garment or so, and he benignly accepted them. By this time the sailors were shouting to us to come aboard, and we took our departure. The ship kept her course: and on the seventh day we reached Alexandria."

Helen Waddell

Mesopotamia in 1917

by

Sir Arnold Wilson, K.C.I.E., C.S.I., C.M.G., D.S.O.

SO close was the regimental bond of fellowship that when, in 1917, a draft from the 32nd Pioneers chanced to halt in Basra below my office window, I instantly recognized, in the confused hum of conversation, the typical accent of my old comrades, and with mounting pulse dashed out to greet them. It was one of the great moments of my life: the regimental dialect, which I had not spoken or even heard for ten years, came back to me, and with it the name of practically every officer, non-commissioned officer, and man there present who had served in the regiment with me. For a few moments I spoke to them in their own tongue as one possessed: a shout arose from their ranks, " Sat Sriwah Guruji ki fateh! Sat Sriwah Guruji ka Khalsa!"—the Sikh war-cry,[1] followed by the shout, " Come back to us! Come with us! Lead us to victory! " The tears flowed down my cheeks. I fled from them for a time, and later in the day begged my chief to let me return to military duty, for which I was now fit. He decided otherwise, but it was long before there faded from my mind the memory of those moments of exaltation and passionate longing to return to the pit from which I was digged and the rock from which I was hewn.

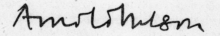

---

[1] The more usual form of the Sikh war-cry is :
" Wâh Guru ji ke khalsa
Äte Wah Guru ji ke fateh
Sât siri Akāl."

England and India :
the Earliest Link

by

Sir Leonard Woolley

A GREAT deal has been written about the con-
nexions between East and West, about the cultural
influences originating in Asia which have affected
European civilization, and those which, working in the
opposite direction, have modified with Western ideals the
indigenous art of the East. Sometimes we can see how
this interchange was effected, how trade or war and invasion
have brought the continents into touch. The great Persian
Empire, stretching to the Mediterranean, carried the crafts
of the age-old Asiatic civilizations to Greece. The conquests of Alexander the Great, the Hellenistic kingdoms
which resulted from his conquests, spread Greek fashions
to Merv and to the Punjab. But there are times when
history fails us ; we see the evidence of contact, but cannot
explain it.

To many English people the monument of Stonehenge,
whose circle of huge stones dominates Salisbury Plain,
appeals as being peculiarly British. They know very little
about Stonehenge: they identify it vaguely, and incor-
rectly, as a Druidic Sun Temple, but they are not greatly
interested in its history. Stonehenge in its isolated gran-
deur, with its massive strength and air of mystery, somehow
symbolizes for them what they like to think are essentially
British qualities; therefore Stonehenge must be essentially
and peculiarly British. In the same spirit of exclusive
ownership they look on other British megalithic monuments, such as Kit's Coty House and Wayland Smith's
cave, as things which you could not expect to find anywhere
but in England.

Of course this is a mistake. England has no monopoly

of such monuments. Jersey can show a megalithic tomb far
finer than any preserved on this side of the Channel.
Stonehenge itself is but a minor version of the huge Carnac
' temple ' in Brittany, whose avenues of approach make
even those of Avebury look small. But megalithic monuments go much farther afield than that: they can be traced
to Spain, to Malta, and across Asia, and nowhere are they
so numerous as in Southern India. So far from being
unique, things whose possession distinguishes England
from other lands, Stonehenge and Wayland Smith's cave
and the like, are links in a chain which binds together
England and India.

It is true that India can boast no single megalithic monument so striking as Stonehenge, but in the number of its
prehistoric relics India is infinitely more rich. It is in
central and south India that they most abound.

Overlooking the city of Hyderabad is a long ridge of
open downland the grassy surface of which is covered with
stone circles, rings twenty or twenty-five feet in diameter
of rough unhewn boulders. The stones were the revet-
ment of earthen cairns—the tumuli or barrows of British
archaeology—and the wind that sweeps over the downs has
carried off the heaped soil and left the stones. Each ring
marks a grave.

On the first hillock that we visited there were over two
hundred such rings in the space of five acres, so Dr
Yazdani, the Director of Archaeology for the State of
Hyderabad, told us; but the range runs on for twelve
miles, and the ancient cemetery extends over the whole of
it. Two of the graves had been excavated, thanks to the
initiative of a former British Resident. At the bottom of
the pit which the cairn had crowned was a stone cist, or
chamber, whose walls were formed of great slabs of stone
measuring about twelve feet by ten, set on edge, while
another slab or slabs made the flat roof. At one end was
a small hole through which offerings could be put. Inside
the chamber the bones of the dead man were found undis-
turbed, and by them were the clay vases which had con-
tained the dead man's meed of food and drink.

Our English dolmens are chamber-tombs just of this sort. They are built on the ground surface and covered with piled-up earth, which in most cases has been denuded by wind and rain so that the sepulchral chamber is to-day exposed above ground; but in their purpose and in their structure they are identical with those of Southern India.

The resemblance is there, and cannot be merely accidental, but we cannot yet explain it; we have not the knowledge that would justify us in basing any theories on what seems so tantalizingly obvious. It is clear that the two sets of monuments belong to one and the same phase in the history of human development—they belong alike to the Later Stone Age—but we cannot therefore say that they are contemporary. To the Late Stone Age in Britain we can assign approximate limits in time; but we do not know the date of the Indian tomb-chambers. Undoubtedly they are old; they go back beyond the scope of human memory. Just as in England megalithic monuments are often associated by name or by local legend with fairies or with the devil, occasionally with a pagan god, such as Wayland, or with a half-historical, half-legendary character, such as King Arthur, so too in India many of the sites where these prehistoric cemeteries are found bear names compounded with the name of the Pandavas, the historic peoples of the Indian epics, who lived at least as long ago as 1500 B.C. It is a fact not without significance, and it gives us a presumption of antiquity; if it could be accepted as evidence it would bring the Indian monuments into a direct time relation with those of Britain; but it is no more than a presumption, and we should hesitate to base a chronology upon it.

Even if we could date accurately one of the South Indian tombs—which we have no means of doing—it would not necessarily solve the problem of the date of the cemeteries generally. For it is possible,—and the mere number of the graves to be found in Southern India suggests this—that the period during which the stone chamber-tombs were built was a very long one, much longer than the period covered by our British dolmens. Beginning in a remote antiquity, it may have continued into times which in other countries we should no longer call prehistoric. India is a land where old customs die hard, and if no political upheaval came to break the tradition a thousand years might pass, or two thousand years, and see little change in the funeral rites of the people. The Stone-Age type of burial may have persisted after the Stone Age ceased, whenever that was. Just as at Stonehenge, the latest in date of Britain's megalithic monuments, we can see how a metal tool has been used to shape the tenons that held the lintel-stones in place, so sometimes in India, as, for example, in the big Chingleput graveyard near Madras, the great stones have been trimmed with metal tools. Therefore, some of the Indian monuments belong at least to the latest phase of the Indian Stone Age, and may come later still in time.

Yet, the use of metal tools does not necessarily make for modernity, because we do not know at all when in Southern India metal-working began. We do know that there was no Bronze Age such as in Europe succeeded the Age of Stone. South India advanced at one bound from flint to iron. But when it made that advance there is nothing to show. We can identify old ironworks, so old that the tools used in ironworking were flints, and the pottery was hand-made and of prehistoric type; but we cannot date them in terms of years. It may be that in Southern India the Stone Age lingered on long after men in other lands had discarded their flint tools in favour of bronze. On the other hand, it may be that the change came early and that Southern Indians were the world's first iron-smiths, and so, fighting their way north, with their better weapons, carried the first-fruits of their own culture to the Ganges and the Indus.

Up till now the study of India's archaeological remains has done little more than present us with problems, and before we can solve them a great deal of work has to be done. Let us be content therefore with stating the problem. In England and in India and in the lands between there are monuments associated in each case with the flint tools and crude hand-made pottery of the childhood of the race, monuments which serve the same ritual purposes and are in their style and method of construction almost identical. These must originate from some common tradition, must bear witness to some cultural relation between peoples so widely separated in space and not necessarily contemporary one with another. What was that relation? What was the link between prehistoric India and prehistoric Britain? Who was responsible for a culture which, as our evidence proves, spread across half the world when the world was young?

Leonard Woolley

The Indian Comforts Fund

The Work done at India House, Aldwych

INDIA HOUSE? Yes, lady, get off at Aldwych. It's the big house with the elephants taking care of it. Can't miss it." That is what you hear if you travel by any of the buses going up the Strand to Fleet Street. . . . We can be proud indeed of our home in this great city. It compares well with the homes of the Dominions close by. We can almost imagine the elephant guardians lifting their trunks in salutation as we pass into the hall— so uniquely conceived. On the walls are frescoes, the work of young Indian artists—one a village boy from Bengal trained in the Ganguli-Tagore Art School at Calcutta. If we look down through the well on the first floor we see in better perspective the tessellated device below, showing the arms of the Provinces of India as the signs of the zodiac.

This view, from above, is equally happy when we walk along to the reading-room of the library and look over the gallery railing into what was used as a reception room at the High Commissioner's parties, before the war.

It was in this room that the Indian Prisoners-of-war Food Packing Centre was inaugurated by Mr Amery, the Secretary of State, on February 4, 1941. It was a day not to be forgotten. Indian and English women sat in the hall packing parcels for the troops, packing deftly—we know the deftness of Indian hands—and quickly, as if by magic, but without haste or fuss. They looked charming in their lovely sarees, as the English women looked no less fittingly garbed in their sombre business clothes.

Mr Amery explained the reason for the Fund which was inaugurated in December 1939. The Government cannot give war moneys for charities like the Red Cross and St John; these must depend on private subscriptions. But the funds in aid of Indian troops were naturally less well known here than the older appeals. So the President had conceived the idea of a special fund. The Chairman is

Mrs Amery, who succeeded Lady Chelmsford in control of the work at India House for Indian soldiers. We are accustomed in India to hearing great British Proconsuls associate their wives with themselves in the services they seek to render our country; and it was always a fresh cause for wonder to Orthodox Hindu Purdahnashoins (secluded women) that this should be so, because of our so different ancient tradition. The tribute was similarly generous on all occasions. But maybe we remember specially the words which Lord Willingdon used and continued to use till he went from our sight, about the partnership of his wife in his work for the Commonwealth.

Mr Amery's tribute was unique in its simplicity. Referring to our Chairman, he said just, " I have personal experience of her efficiency." And, indeed, so have we all at India House. And not of efficiency alone, but of the royal gift which recognizes individuals and makes each worker feel as if she were of specially needed service to the cause served by all; self-effacing and able to delegate authority —the sign of true leadership—India House workers affectionately call her " the little mother."

The committee room is the office. In this busy building —exquisitely panelled with our precious Indian timbers— it is perhaps the busiest room of all. Mrs Amery, the Secretary, Colonel Shepherd, and the Treasurer, our old friend Sir Henry Wheeler, sit at their desks behind screens, but accessible to every one. What impresses the visitor is the cheerfulness and courtesy with which all workers alike face interruptions. We all know the annoyance caused by intrusion upon concentrated work. Is it not made classic by Byron's response to his wife's, " Dearest, do I interrupt you? "—" Yes—damnably! " The honorary workers at India House—from Chairman to the humblest packer— must often have felt that word. We've never heard it! Lady Wheeler, Mrs Mills, Lady Stephenson, Lady Maccaw, Miss Goodfellow, and others known to us in India work here, with Indians among whom Mrs Lall is a familiar figure.

Try to picture the scene. One worker is unpacking and sorting the garments sent from working parties, and also from India—pullovers, helmets, sea-stockings, socks, gloves, scarves, all beautifully made—though another worker scrutinizes every garment, tidying, for example, the loose ends which sometimes appear in the touching gifts sent out by invalids and the aged; others are weighing and making records of the wool purchased or sent to workers, sorting, storing. . . . Messenger boys handle the incoming and outgoing parcels, tossing them with the expert skill of workers in a city warehouse. Indians will like to know that some of the sea-boot stockings received at India House come from Kalimpong, and are of wool spun and knitted there. The room where we used to await our friends in the old days is where prisoners' clothing and comforts parcels are packed. We purchase our needs for prisoners of war through the Red Cross, and our old Delhi friend, Sir Ernest Burdon, is Deputy Chairman at the London Headquarters of the British Red Cross and St John Joint War Organization. Busy packing is going on in this section also. But the most popular department of all seems to be the Indian Food Packing Centre for Prisoners of War. The majority of the Indian workers and English women work here together. The Indians you have probably seen in the pictures published from time to time in the newspapers. The English women are never shown in the photographs, but they include not only ' ex-Indians ' (wives of retired officials), but English women for whom India House is their first association with India. How greatly the magnificent contribution of our fighting men to the common cause has impressed this country was demonstrated lately when a broadcast appeal for help brought in some eight hundred new work parties, varying from a minimum of six to whole schools most of whom were already knitting for other funds. The Fund now numbers 100,000 knitters.

But there is yet another side to the work done at India House. Every Tuesday afternoon the men of the Indian Forces now in England, whether on leave or service, are entertained at tea. They represent castes and races from various parts of India; and the value of this comradeship of service was illustrated one day in what one of the soldiers said to a worker. The men sit at little tables and are waited upon by the workers, those knowing the vernacular moving from table to table to sit awhile beside the men and talk to them. Answering a question one day from a worker as to where the men came from, "Both from the North-West Frontier," said the man on her left; "I am a Mochi [leather-worker]." "And I," added the man on her right, "a Zemindar [Brahmin landowner], both made brothers by the service of our Badshah Bahadur." Caste and outside caste Hindu sitting side by side eating and *drinking*—we know the implication of that latter—food served by non-Hindus! At other tables one found Hindu and Moslem equally placed. Such facts need no comment.

H.M. the Queen, H.R.H. the Duchess of Gloucester, H.R.H. the Duchess of Kent, and H.H. Princess Marie Louise have visited India House to see and encourage the workers. Of the gracious, lovely words spoken by Her Majesty, and the personal interest taken as always on her visits to war workers, you have already heard in India, and have doubtless felt encouraged in the work done in India for the same object.

The Queen Mother, H.M. Queen Mary, now lives outside London and cannot visit us, but her interest has been shown by a generous donation to the Fund, and by the gracious permission to let this book bear her name. It will be sold for the Indian Comforts Fund. The service rendered has been honorary throughout so that all royalties may go to the Fund. The Book is unique for a publication of its kind, since it is really a tribute to the Indian war effort in all directions.

NOTE

One final word cannot be forborne of abiding gratitude to Lady (Bruce) Richmond, who has been throughout the preparation of this book the Indian Editor's most efficient and encouraging partner in this labour of love.

Extract from the Chairman's Broadcast
to India of November 26, 1941

OUR endeavour is to give help, happiness, comfort, and interest to Indian soldiers, sailors, seamen, and others who are here, and to all Indians who are prisoners of war. We work at India House. That is our centre, but throughout these islands thousands of women are knitting woollen articles of all kinds. They knit for the British Army, Navy, and Air Force, but they knit too for Indian soldiers and sailors. From Australia, South Africa, Canada, New Zealand, and Rhodesia presents come to us for Indians, gifts of comforts and gifts of money. From India House these comforts flow out in a steady stream to the men who want them, prepared and packed by Indian and English ladies, and we are happy to receive information through the Red Cross from German prison camps telling us how greatly the men appreciate the weekly food parcels and the regular supply of woollen comforts. . . .

It is not possible to tell you of the volume of good-will and kindness that goes with this work. The women of England whose sons are serving overseas can understand and sympathize with the plight of men who are so far from their homes, living in such different surroundings and in such a different climate, and they are anxious to help.

Sir Firozkhan Noon, until recently High Commissioner for India in England, is now in India, and I am sure he will tell anyone who is interested about our work. The women of England can sympathize with the women of India because they too have sons, husbands, and brothers serving overseas. They too live anxious days—no words are necessary to explain that understanding; it is in the hearts of us all.

Indian Comforts Fund Statistics

LIEUTENANT-COLONEL C. SHEPHERD, D.S.O.

PATRONS : The Secretary of State for India, the Right Hon.
L. S. Amery, P.C., M.P. The High Commissioner for
India, Sir M. Azizul Huque, C.I.E.

PRESIDENT : The Dowager-Viscountess Chelmsford, G.B.E.,
C.I.

CHAIRMAN : Mrs L. S. Amery.

HON. TREASURER : Sir Henry Wheeler, K.C.S.I., K.C.I.E.

HON. SECRETARY : Lieutenant-Colonel C. Shepherd.

We give here some indication of the work undertaken by
the Fund.

For Prisoners-of-War or Internees. Three thousand parcels
are dispatched weekly in bulk to Geneva for distribution
to men of all Services who are imprisoned or interned in
Germany, France, or Italy.

Duties of next-of-kin are also undertaken within the
regulations—*i.e.* the dispatch of 3000 quarterly parcels
of clothing and comforts.

For the Royal Indian Navy. Warm clothing, comforts,
games, and recreational facilities are supplied to the Royal
Indian Navy as opportunity offers.

For Indian Seamen. It is estimated that between 30,000
and 40,000 Indian seamen of the Indian Merchant Service
call at our ports yearly. Each man gets a parcel of clothing and comforts suited to needs of deck, saloon, and
engine-room crews. Distribution is carried out through
Seamen Welfare Officers. Hostels and boarding-houses on
shore are helped by grants of money and provision for
shower-baths, radiograms, books, etc.

For the Indian Contingent and Pioneer Corps stationed in England. Warm clothing, comforts, games, and recreational facilities are provided. Outings are organized for leave parties, and help given generally.

General Help. To Indian soldiers and sailors in hospitals in England help is given in a variety of ways. Contact is made on their behalf with individuals in the Ministry of Labour and in Government Training Centres. The Fund provides also for the relief of Indians in any position who may be in distress.

Working Parties. There are 1683 working parties in England, Wales, and Scotland with a total membership of 100,000 knitters, to whom wool is supplied free by the Fund. Working parties are required to return the equivalent weight of wool in knitted garments.